ALSO FROM THE MODERN LIBRARY GARDENING SERIES

Old Herbaceous by Reginald Arkell

We Made a Garden by Margery Fish

The Gardener's Year by Karel Čapek

In the Land of the Blue Poppies by Frank Kingdon Ward

Green Thoughts by Eleanor Perényi

My Summer in a Garden by Charles Dudley Warner

The Gardener's Bed-Book by Richardson Wright

THE AMERICAN
GARDENER

William Cobbett

The American Gardener

A Treatise on the

SITUATION, SOIL, AND LAYING OUT OF GARDENS,

ON THE MAKING AND MANAGING OF HOT- BEDS
AND GREEN-HOUSES;

AND

ON THE PROPAGATION AND CULTIVATION OF
THE SEVERAL SORTS OF

**VEGETABLES, HERBS, FRUITS,
AND FLOWERS.**

Michael Pollan
Series Editor

Introduction by Verlyn Klinkenborg

THE MODERN LIBRARY

NEW YORK

The text of this Modern Library edition of *The American Gardener* was set
from an 1856 edition published by C. M. Saxton & Company, no. 14 Fulton
Street, New York City. Minor errors have been silently corrected.

LIBRARY OF CONGRESS CATALOGING-IN-PUBLICATION DATA
Cobbett, William, 1763–1835.
The American gardener / William Cobbett ; introduction
by Verlyn Klinkenborg.—
Modern library ed.
p. cm.—(Modern Library gardening series)
ISBN 0-8129-6737-2
1. Gardening—United States. I. Title. II. Series.

SB453 .C613 2003
635'.0973—dc21   2002038027

Modern Library website address:
www.modernlibrary.com

Printed in the United States of America

2 4 6 8 9 7 5 3 1

Contents

INTRODUCTION TO THE MODERN LIBRARY
  GARDENING SERIES *by Michael Pollan*   ix
INTRODUCTION *by Verlyn Klinkenborg*   xiii
PREFACE   xxiii

THE AMERICAN GARDENER

  I. ON THE SITUATION, SOIL, FENCING, AND
     LAYING-OUT OF GARDENS   3
 II. ON THE MAKING AND MANAGING OF HOT-BEDS
     AND GREEN-HOUSES   29
III. ON PROPAGATION AND CULTIVATION IN GENERAL   56
 IV. VEGETABLES AND HERBS   88
  V. FRUITS   147
 VI. FLOWERS   186

INDEX TO VEGETABLES AND HERBS, FRUITS AND FLOWERS   211
INDEX TO THE GENERAL MATTER   215

Introduction to the Modern Library Gardening Series

Michael Pollan

It took a woodchuck and a book to make me understand what's really at stake in the garden.

I'd come to gardening in the naïve belief it offered a fairly benign way to kill an afternoon, a refuge from the wider world, but even before the end of my first season I'd been forcibly relieved of my innocence. First came the rodent. A series of increasingly desperate measures to run a hungry woodchuck out of my vegetable patch escalated into a personal Vietnam (with me in the role of General Westmoreland, fully prepared to destroy the garden in order to save it), which promptly exploded the whole "garden-as-refuge" concept. The spectacle of my own rodenticidal rage suggested that more was involved in gardening than tending a few tomatoes and prettifying my yard. It put one into a relationship with nature that was anything but innocent.

But it wasn't until I cracked open Eleanor Perényi's *Green Thoughts,* a tart, smart, and beautifully written set of alphabetical essays (from "Annuals" to "Woman's Place") published in 1981, that I realized how much was really going on here, right under my nose.

Perényi had found in the garden everything from sexual politics and class struggle to culinary fashion and, particularly relevant to my woodchuck problem, ecological insight. The garden, in other words, was better approached as an arena than a refuge, an idea I immediately seized on and have yet to let go of. Though I suspect neither party would especially appreciate the tribute, I can trace the discovery of my own vocation as a writer to the crossing, in 1984 or thereabouts, of that particular book with that particular rodent.

What Perényi had done was to introduce me to an unexpectedly rich, provocative, and frequently uproarious conversation that, metaphorically at least, takes place over the back fence that joins any two gardens in the world. Was there really such a thing as a green thumb? (Nonsense, said Perényi; why of course! countered Russell Page.) Was I within my rights to firebomb a woodchuck burrow? (Don't answer.) Must we concede the moral superiority of native species? And why is it magenta is so often maligned? (All too common, huffs Alice Morse Earle, before Louise Beebe Wilder leaps to its defense.) From book to book, across oceans and centuries, the horticultural backing-and-forthing unfolds with such urgency you'd be forgiven for thinking the fence of space and time were merely picket.

Right away I wanted in on the conversation, and, handed off from one writer to the next, soon made the acquaintance of a crowd of fine and fiercely opinionated talkers. There was Karel Čapek, a gimlet-eyed Czech who relished the human comedy he found in the garden, and Margery Fish, a gentle Englishwoman whose cottage garden in Somerset told the story of a marriage. Closer to home, there was Katharine White in Maine, reading her January harvest of seed catalogues as a species of literature; Charles Dudley Warner in Hartford, setting himself up as the Mark Twain of American horticulture; and Alice Morse Earle in Massachusetts bringing an almost Jamesian regard to the social swirl of her perennial border. (The peony, Earle wrote, "always looks like a well-dressed, well-shod, well-gloved girl of birth, breeding, and of equal good taste and good health; a girl who can swim and hike and play golf. . . .")

Most of these essayists were moonlighting in the garden, which usually meant they were fired with the enthusiasm of the amateur and the liberty of the writer cultivating a piece of ground some distance from literature's main thoroughfares. Their voices could be by turns personal and prescriptive, diffident and prickly, and, somehow, both self-deprecating and incontrovertible at the same time. Since these writers often came to the subject from elsewhere, they were particularly good at drawing unexpected lines of connection between what was going on in their gardens and the seemingly distant realms of politics, art, sex, class, even morality. I discovered that as soon as one got past the how-to volumes written by experts, and the illustrated coffee-table tomes of garden porn, the garden bookshelf brimmed with the sort of quirky, sui generis writing often produced by a good mind operating in a small space.

And so I read to garden, and gardened to read, counting myself lucky for having stumbled on a sideline with such a lively and lasting literature. For what other pastime has spawned so many fine books? Only fly-fishing comes even close. (Numismatics? Woodworking? Macrame? Come on!) Which is probably no accident: for gardening, like angling, engages us with the natural world, as actors rather than passive spectators. Both put us smack on the frontier between nature and culture, which is always an interesting place for a writer to stand. And both literary traditions pose practical and philosophical questions about how we might better go about rhyming our desires with nature's ways, questions that only grow more urgent with time.

The books I've chosen for this series are the classics that form the backbone of this tradition. What you won't find on this particular shelf are reference works and strictly how-to books; there's plenty of how-to here, but the emphasis is more along the lines of how-to-think-about-it than how-to-do-it. Even the oldest among them will be contemporary in the best sense, offering a still-vibrant voice in the back-fence conversation gardeners have been conducting at least since the time of Pliny. I'm not sure whether or not we should be surprised by this, but a great many of the issues that engaged Pliny are the same ones that centuries later would engage Alexander Pope and Vita Sackville-West, Gertrude Jekyll and Eleanor Perényi, Charles Dudley Warner and Karel Čapek, and will no doubt engage gardeners centuries hence. I'm thinking of the power of plants to change us in mind and body, the gratuitous beauty of a flower, the moral lessons of the pest, the ancient language of landscape design, and the endlessly engrossing ways that cultivating a garden attaches a body to the earth.

Introduction

Verlyn Klinkenborg

On April 18, 1818, William Cobbett—a fifty-five-year-old Englishman living on a farm in North Hempstead, Long Island—wrote in his journal, "We have *sprouts* from the cabbage stems preserved under cover; the Swedish turnip is giving me *greens* from bulbs planted out in March; and I have some *broccoli* too, just coming on for use. *How* I have got this broccoli I must explain in my *Gardener's Guide;* for write one I must. I can never leave this country without an attempt to make every farmer a gardener."

In this journal entry, Cobbett was, as always, making a point. He did write a Gardener's Guide, which you are holding, called *The American Gardener,* first published in London in 1821. (A version of this book revised for an English audience and called *The English Gardener* was published in 1828.) If you look up "Dandelion," you'll find this apparently peripheral note: "In the spring (June) 1817, when I came to Long Island, and when nothing in the shape of *greens* was to be had for love or money, *Dandelions* were our resource; and I have always, since that time, looked at this *weed* with a more friendly eye." Cobbett's point is this: Once settled, he managed to have greens by April. The rest of Long Island could grow none by June. The secret? Hot-beds.

This is Cobbett all over: two parts practical knowledge, two parts rural economy—and one part self-satisfaction, a pleasure it's hard to begrudge him. A quick sketch of just who and what Cobbett was when he decided "to make every farmer a gardener" will allow you to enjoy his self-satisfaction too. Cobbett came to America in 1817 in what he called "self-banishment," fleeing the wrath of an English government that had recently suspended habeas corpus in order to imprison its enemies more easily. Cobbett was arguably the most important of them. By 1817, he had been writing *Cobbett's Weekly Political Register,* the only politically independent newspaper in England, for fifteen years, and he would continue to write it until a week before his death in 1835. That paper, published every Saturday, was the voice of political reform, and "among the great mass of people it became the most powerful journal in England," according to Cobbett's chief biographer, George Spater.

Cobbett had lived in the New World before 1817: He'd come to New Brunswick in 1785 as a soldier. After his discharge and marriage in England, and a short stint in France, he returned with his wife, Nancy, to Philadelphia in 1792, "passing," as he says, "eight years there, becoming bookseller and author, and taking a prominent part in all the important discussions of the interesting period from 1793 to 1799, during which there was, in that country, a continual struggle carried on between the English and the French parties." Those vitriolic "discussions" were in ink. Cobbett's American pseudonym was Peter Porcupine, and his vehicle was *Porcupine's Gazette*—in nearly all respects but one, a precursor to *Cobbett's Weekly Political Register.* That one respect was the side he took.

Before 1800 and his return to England, Cobbett was an archconservative, a member of the English party in Philadelphia trying to bring about closer ties between America and its parent country, a relationship still in tatters after the American Revolution and made far worse by the havoc of the French Revolution and its consequences. But at home in England, Cobbett found a corrupt government, a failing monetary policy, a venal Parliament, and a collapsing agriculture. He made a volte-face of stunning proportions and passed it off as consistency. He began to view the "weed" America, like the dandelion, with a more friendly eye. He began to clamor for reform of Parliament, to campaign against a national debt and a paper money that was bankrupting farmers and destroying the lives of farm laborers. And when he faced the near certainty of being imprisoned by the English government—it would have been his second political incarceration—he boarded ship with two of his sons and made America his refuge until the end of 1819.

This is the person you must imagine as you begin to read *The American Gardener,* nearly as famous a man as there was at the time in England or America. He is already, as William Hazlitt said in 1821, "unquestionably the most powerful political writer of the present day," and he is on the cusp of becoming, as Hazlitt also put it, "one of the best writers in the language." For, in fact, the great period of Cobbett's work is about to begin. If Cobbett ever lay fallow, it was in the grave.

While he was in America, living on Long Island, Cobbett kept up his political barrage in the pages of the *Political Register.* On December 6, 1817, he began writing *A Grammar of the English Language, in a Series of Letters,* which was published in New York the following year. It is, as Hazlitt affirms, "as entertaining as a story-book," and it sold 100,000 copies by 1834 and remained in print at least until 1919, a fact that is all the more amazing when you remember that Cobbett began life as a plowboy. He wrote and published *A Year's Residence in the United States of America* and began work on *The American Gardener.* Still ahead lay some of his greatest books, published in quick succession in the early 1820s: *Cottage Economy;* a French grammar that was no less successful than his English grammar; *A History of the Protestant Reformation;* and the first of the essays that became *Rural Rides,* a masterpiece of political and agricultural reporting.

—

It may sound as though Cobbett had been dipped in printer's ink at birth and baptized with political ichor. But he was the child of a farm laborer and grew up in Hampshire during a period of genuine agricultural prosperity. He had as many ideas as there were minutes in his day, which always began at four A.M. "He is like a young and lusty bridegroom," Hazlitt wrote, "that divorces a favourite speculation every morning, and marries a new one every night. He is not wedded to his notions, not he. He has not one Mrs. Cobbett among all his opinions." But there was a Mrs. Cobbett among his sentiments, and that was a love of the land, of farming, of gardening, and of the virtues of a prosperous rural life, no matter how poor in outward show.

Practically the only time in his life when Cobbett did not have his hands in the soil was during the two years (1810–12) he spent imprisoned in Newgate, and even then he gardened by proxy, receiving daily reports and samples of home produce in baskets sent by his children and sending instructions in return. He established a nursery, shipping seeds and grafts to and from America. He started an experimental farm where he grew Swedish turnips, mangel-wurzel, and maize. (He also wrote a book called *Corn: A Treatise on Cobbett's Corn* [1828].) By 1825, Cobbett is said by George Spater to have "planted a million forest trees and about 10,000 apple trees." If he had been a prudent man, financially, he might also have been a rich one.

Cobbett found that America in 1817 was *"a country of farmers."* But it was also a country where the sheer abundance of land overwhelmed any desire to garden on a single spot. "When large parcels of land are undertaken to be cultivated," Cobbett writes in the Preface to *The American Gardener,* "small ones are held in contempt; and, though a good garden supplies so large a part of what is consumed by a family, and keeps supplying it all the year round too, there are many farmers even in England, who grudge even a wheelbarrow full of manure that is bestowed on the garden." Cobbett's purpose in *The American Gardener* is nothing less than to teach the rudiments of gardening to American farmers and to inculcate in them the love of cottage gardens found among rural laborers in the England of Cobbett's youth.

As you read *The American Gardener*, do not let yourself picture Cobbett seated at a desk, pen in hand, during the light of the day. Imagine, instead, that it is early, early morning, and that he is dictating to one of his children before the sun comes up. After four hours of literary work, he turns to other business. He had taken over a long-abandoned house on Long Island, and he and his children restored the garden there. He raised pigs, oxen, chickens, sheep, ducks, and turkeys. And when that house burned down in the spring of 1819, he raised a tent, lined it with English newspapers, and camped out there for several months, dressed in "a shirt, a pair of nankin trowsers, yellow buckskin shoes & a broad-brimmed straw hat."

What does a modern American gardener make of *The American Gardener*? For one thing, nearly all the advice is still good advice. It's impossible to improve, for instance, on Cobbett's description of how to prepare the soil for planting: "Make the ground rich, move it deep, and make it fine." He walks you through the double-digging of a garden plot, a task that hasn't changed since 1821. With the manure of cattle or horses and a little effort, you could still make a hotbed of the kind Cobbett describes, following his instructions to the letter, and it would yield just as Cobbett says it does. No one has ever written a better or clearer description of how to eat an artichoke. And if Cobbett's passions overflow from time to time—as they always did—they are excellent passions. To him, the locust (*Robinia pseudocacia*) is the "most beautiful of trees and best of timber." To him, sea kale "is, unquestionably, (after the Asparagus,) the very best garden vegetable that grows." The geranium (the pelargonium, that is) "wants *hardiness only* to make it the finest flower-plant of which I have any knowledge." The cranberry "is one of the best fruits in the world. All tarts sink out of sight in point of merit, when compared with that made of the American Cranberry."

In *The American Gardener*, Cobbett proposes an ideal garden, built from scratch on new ground, as befits America in the early nineteenth century. His ideal is almost exactly the size of a football field, one hundred yards by fifty yards, surrounded by a living hawthorn fence that's tight enough to keep out a sucking pig or a boy after orchard fruit and tall enough to deter poultry. In almost every particular, Cobbett urges the gardener to consider the neatness, the handsomeness, with which he does things. Partly, this is for moral reasons. "Poverty may apologize," he writes, "for a dirty dress or an unshaven face; men may be negligent of their persons; but the sentence of the whole nation is, that he, who is a sloven in his garden, is a sloven indeed. The inside of a labourer's house, his habits, his qualities as a workman, and almost his morality, may be judged of from the appearance of his garden."

But Cobbett also urges neatness and beauty for practical reasons too. "Next comes *the act of sowing*," he writes. "The more *handsomely* this is done, the *better* it is done. A handsome dress is *better* than an ugly one, not because it is warmer, or cooler, but because, liking it better, being more pleased with it, we *take more care of it*." And, besides, Cobbett imagines the American farmer building a garden for the ages. When it comes to laying out the hawthorn hedge, "place *a line along very truly;* for, mind, you are planting for generations to come!" He describes how to make a rakelike tool for laying out drills, or rows, in the soil. If made, as he recommends, with white oak for the head and locust for the teeth, "every body knows, that the tools might descend from father to son to the fourth or fifth generation."

You may not choose to garden directly from the pages of *The American Gardener*, though generations of gardeners have done so. But in these pages you will find another America, a place where the abundance of wild huckleberries on Long Island "gives rise to a *holiday,* called *Huckleberry Monday,*" where fine laburnums bloom "between *Brooklyn* and the Turnpike gate." And, best of all, you will find a rich helping of the genuine Cobbett. Thomas Carlyle described him as "the pattern John Bull of his century, strong as the rhinoceros, and with singular humanities and genialities shining through his thick skin." He is a man of genuine tenderness. "For, count our real pleasures," he writes; "count the things that delight us through life: and you will find, that ninety-nine out of every hundred are derived from women. To be the object of *no woman's* care or good wishes is a sentence the most severe that can be pronounced upon man."

And even if you don't end up making a hot-bed or planting a hawthorn hedge, you'll still find yourself going down to the garden with Cobbett's words in mind: "Seasons wait for no man. Nature makes us her offers freely; but she will be taken at her word."

—

VERLYN KLINKENBORG is a *New York Times* editorialist and the author of *The Rural Life, The Last Fine Time,* and *Making Hay.* He lives in Austerlitz, New York.

Preface.

1.

The proper uses of a Preface appear to be, to give the reader information, which may be useful, during the perusal of the work to which it is prefixed; to explain the nature and object of the work; to point out the method of the arrangement of its several parts; and, in short, to afford the means of due preparation for the task the reader is entering upon; which preparation is always a great advantage to the author as well as to the reader.

2.

As to the *nature* of the work, it is, I hope, pretty clearly stated in the Title Page. The *object* evidently is to cause the art of gardening to be better understood and practised than it now is in America; and, very few persons will deny, that there is, in this case, plenty of room for improvement. America has soil and climate far surpassing those of England; and yet she is surprizingly deficient in variety as well as quality of garden products. I am not alluding to things of *ornament,* or appertaining to *luxurious* enjoyments; but, to things that are really useful, and that tend to profit and to the preservation of health, without which latter, life is not worth having. It is incredible to those, who have not had occasion to observe the fact, how large a part of the sustenance of a country-labourer's family, in England, comes out of his little garden. The labourers of England are distinguished from those of other countries by several striking peculiarities; but, by no one are they so strongly distinguished as by their fondness of their gardens, and by the diligence, care and taste, which they show in the management of them. The reproach which Solomon, in the words of my motto, affixes on the slothful and ignorant husbandman, they seem to have constantly in their minds; and to be constantly on the watch to prevent it from applying to themselves. Poverty may apologize for a dirty dress or an unshaven face; men may be negligent of their persons; but the sentence of the whole nation is, that he, who is a sloven in his garden, is a sloven indeed. The inside of a labourer's house, his habits, his qualities as a workman, and almost his morality, may be judged of from the appearance of his garden. If that be neglected, he is, nine times out of ten, a sluggard or a drunkard, or both.

3.

It seems, at first sight, very odd that this taste for gardening should not have been preserved in America; but, it is accounted for by reflecting, that where land is abundant, attachment and even attention to *small spots* wear away. To desire to possess land is a universal desire; and vanity makes us prefer quantity to quality. You may prove as clearly as daylight, that it is better, in certain cases, to possess one acre than a hundred; but where do you find the man that prefers the one acre? When large parcels of land are undertaken to be cultivated, small ones are held in contempt; and, though a good garden supplies so large a part of what is consumed by a family, and keeps supplying it all the year round too, there are many farmers even in England, who grudge even a wheelbarrow full of manure that is bestowed on the garden. To remove this neglect as to gardening in America is one of the objects of this work;

and, I think, I shall, in the progress of the work, show, that the garden may, besides its intrinsic utility, be made to be a most valuable helpmate to the *Farm.*

4.

It is impossible to write a book that shall exclusively apply to every particular case. Some persons have need of large, while others want only small gardens; but, as to *Situation, Soil,* and *Fencing,* the rules will apply to all cases. Those who want neither *Hot-Beds* nor *Green-Houses,* may read the part treating of them, or leave it unread, just as they please; but, I think, that it will not require much to be said to convince *every American Farmer,* North of Carolina, at least, that he ought to have a Hot-Bed in the Spring.

5.

I have divided the matters, treated of, thus: The *first* Chapter treats of the Situation, Soil, Fencing, and Laying-out of Gardens; the *second,* of the making and managing of Hot-Beds and Green-Houses; the *third,* of Propagation and Cultivation generally; the *three* remaining Chapters treat of the raising and managing of the several plants, each under its particular name, classed under the heads, *Vegetables* and *Herbs; Fruits; Flowers.* In each of these last three Chapters, I have, in arranging my matter, followed the *Alphabetical Order* of the names of the several plants, which mode of arrangement must naturally tend to make the work of *reference* easy. But, as very frequent reference must be necessary, and, as the utility of the work must, in some degree, depend on the *facility* with which the several parts of it can be referred to, there are two Indexes at the end, one of the *names of the several plants,* and, the other, of the matters generally. For the same reason, I have *numbered the paragraphs* throughout the work. A more proper term might have been found than that of *Vegetables,* seeing, that, strictly speaking, that word applies to all things that grow from the earth. But, as we call those products of the garden, which we use, in their natural shape, as human food; as we generally call *these only* by the name of *vegeta-bles*, I have chosen that word in preference to one, which, though more strictly proper, would be less generally understood. Nearly the same may be said of the word *Herbs*.

6.

Some persons may think, that *Flowers* are things of no *use*; that they are *nonsensical* things. The same may be, and, perhaps, with more reason, said of *pictures*. An Italian, while he gives his fortune for a picture, will laugh to scorn a Hollander, who leaves a tulip-root as a fortune to his son. For my part, as a thing to keep and not to sell; as a thing, the *possession* of which is to give me pleasure, I hesitate not a moment to prefer the plant of a fine carnation to a gold watch set with diamonds.

7.

The territory of the United States includes such a variety of climates; degrees of heat and cold so different at the same period of the year; that it is impossible to give instructions, as relating to *time*, for sowing, planting, and so forth, that shall be applicable to every part of the country. I, therefore, for the most part, make my directions applicable to *seasons*, or states of the weather, rather than to *dates*. When I make no particular mention as to times of the year, or month, it is to be understood, that I am supposing myself at, or near, *the City of New York*, and that I am speaking of what ought to be done there. With this clearly borne in mind, the reader, who will know the difference in the degrees of heat and cold in the different parts of the country, will know how to apply the instructions accordingly.

8.

Those persons, who perform their garden work themselves, will need no caution with respect to men that they employ as *Gardeners*; but, those who employ Gardeners ought by no means to *leave them to do as they please.* Their practical experience is worth something; but, if they are generally found very deficient in knowledge of their business in England, what must those of them be who come to America? Every man, who can dig and hoe and rake, calls himself a *Gardener* as soon as he lands here from England. This description of persons are generally *handy men,* and, having been used to spade-work, they, from habit, do things well and neatly. But as to the *art of gardening,* they generally know nothing of it. I wished to carry the nicer parts of gardening to perfection, at Botley. I succeeded. But I took care to employ no man who called himself *a gardener.* I selected handy and clear-headed farm-labourers. They did what I ordered them to do; and offered me none of their *advice* or *opinions.*

9.

There is a foible of human nature, which greatly contributes to establish and perpetuate the power and the mischief of pretended gardeners. Tell a gentleman, that this is wrong, or that is wrong, in the management of his garden, and he instantly and half-angrily replies, that *his gardener is a very skilful man.* "That may be," said I once to a friend, who, at an enormous expense, had got two or three poor little melons, while I, at hardly any expense at all, had large quantities of very fine ones: "That may be," said I, "for skill may consist in getting you to expend your money without getting you any fruit." The truth is, however, that it is not a desire to be deceived, that produces this species of perverseness: it is a desire not to be thought foolish. The gentleman has *chosen the gardener;* and, the reason why he stickles for him is, that, if he allow the gardener to be a bad one, he himself has *made a bad choice;* and that would be an *imputation on his understanding,* rather than allow which to be just, he will cheerfully bleed from his purse pretty freely.

10.

The best security against the effects of this foible of human nature, is, for the owner of the garden to be *head gardener himself;* and,

I hope that this work may assist in rendering this office easy and pleasant. But, to perform the office well, the owner must be *diligent* as well as skilful. He must look *forward*. It is a very good way to look attentively at every part of the garden every Saturday, and to write down some, at least, of the things to be done during the *next week*. This tends to prevent those *omissions*, which, when they have once taken place, are not easily compensated for. Seasons wait for no man. Nature makes us her offers freely; but she will be taken at her word.

11.

I cannot help, in conclusion of this preface, expressing my hope, that this work may tend to the increasing, in some degree, of a taste for gardening in America. It is a source of much greater profit than is generally imagined; and, merely as an amusement, or recreation, it is one of the most rational and most conducive to health. It is a pursuit, not only compatible with, but favourable to, the *study* of any art or science. It tends to turn the minds of youth from amusements and attachments of a frivolous or vicious nature. It is indulged *at home*. It tends to make home pleasant; and to endear to us the spot on which it is our lot to live.

WM. COBBETT.

North Hampstead, Long Island, 1819.

THE AMERICAN
GARDENER

I

On the Situation, Soil, Fencing, and Laying-out of Gardens.

SITUATION.

12.

Those who have gardens already formed and planted, have, of course, not the situation to choose. But, I am to suppose, that new gardens will, in a country like this, be continually to be formed; and, therefore, it is an essential part of my duty to point out what situations are best, as well with respect to the *aspect* as to the other circumstances.

13.

The ground should be as nearly on a *level* as possible; because, if the slope be considerable, the heavy rains do great injury, by washing away the soil. However, it is not always in our power to choose a level spot; but, if there be a slope in the ground, it ought, if possible, to be towards the *South*. For, though such a direction adds to the heat in summer, this is more than counterbalanced by the *earliness* which it causes in the spring. By all means avoid an inclination towards the North, or West, and towards any of the points between

North and West. After all, it may not be in our power to have a level spot, nor even a spot nearly level; and then we must do our best with what we have.

14.

I am speaking here solely of a Kitchen-garden. Of *ornamental* Gardening I shall speak a little in the Chapter on *Flowers*. From a Kitchen-garden all *large trees* ought to be kept at a distance of thirty or forty yards. For, the *shade* of them is injurious, and their *roots* a great deal more injurious, to every plant growing within the influence of those roots. It is a common but very erroneous notion, in England, that the trees, which grow in the hedges that divide the fields, do injury by their *shade only*. I had a field of transplanted Ruta Baga, in the hedge on the North West side of which there were five large spreading oak-trees, at some distance from each other. Opposite each of these trees, which could not *shade* the Ruta Baga much, there was a piece of the Ruta Baga, in nearly a semi-circular form, in which the plants never grew to any size, though those in all the rest of the field were so fine as to draw people from a great distance to look at them. One gentleman, who came out of Sussex, and who had been a farmer all his life-time, was struck with the sight of these semi-circles; and, looking over the hedge, into a field of wheat, which had a *ditch* between it and the hedge, and seeing that the wheat, though *shaded* by the trees, was very little affected by them, he discovered, that it was the *roots* and not the *branches* that produced the mischief. The *ditch,* which had been for ages in the same place, had prevented the roots of the trees from going into the field where the wheat was growing. The ground where the Ruta Baga was growing had been well ploughed and manured; and the plants had not been in the ground more than *three months;* yet, such was the power of the roots of the trees, and so quickly did it operate, that it almost wholly destroyed the Ruta Baga that stood within its reach. *Grass,* which matts the ground all over with its roots, and does not demand much food from any depth, does not suffer much from the roots of trees; but, every other plant does. A Kitchen-garden should, therefore, have no large trees near it. In the spring and fall tall trees do great harm even by their *shade,* which robs the garden of the early and the parting rays of the sun. It is, therefore, on all accounts, desirable to keep all such trees at a distance.

15.

If it be practicable, without sacrificing too much in other respects, to make a garden near to running water, and especially to water that may be turned into the garden, the advantage ought to be profited of; but as to *watering* with a *watering pot,* it is seldom of much use, and it cannot be practised upon a large scale. It is better to trust to judicious tillage and to the dews and rains. The moisture which these do not supply cannot be furnished, to any extent, by the watering-pot. A man will *raise* more moisture, with a hoe or spade, in a day, than he can pour on the earth out of a watering-pot in a month.

SOIL.
16.

The plants, which grow in a garden, prefer, like most other plants, the best soil that is to be found. The best is, loam of several feet deep, with a bed of lime-stone, sand-stone, or sand, below. But, we must take what we *find,* or, rather, what we happen to have. If we have a choice, we ought to take that which comes nearest to perfection, and, if we possibly can, we ought to reject *clay,* and *gravel,* not only as a top soil, but as a bottom soil, however great their distance from the surface. See paragraph 109.

17.

Oak-trees love clay, and the finest and heaviest wheat grows in land with a bottom of clay; but, if there be clay within even six feet of the surface, there will be a *coldness* in the land, which will, in spite of all you can do, keep your spring crops a week or ten days behind those upon land which has not a bottom of clay. *Gravel* is warm, and it would be very desirable, if you could exchange it for some other early in June; but, since you cannot do this, you must submit to be burnt up in summer, if you have the benefit of a gravelly bottom in the spring.

18.

If the land, where you like to have a garden has *rocks*, great or small, they, of course, are to be carried off; but, if you have a *stony* soil, that is to say, little short of *gravel to the very surface*, and, if you can get no other spot, you must e'en hammer your tools to pieces amongst the stones; for it has been amply proved by experience, that to carry away stones of the *flint* or *gravel* kind impoverishes the land. However, we are not to frame out plans upon the supposition of meeting with obstacles of this extraordinary nature. We are not to suppose, that, in a country where men have had to *choose*, and have still *to choose*, they will have built, and yet will build, their houses on spots peculiarly steril. We must suppose the contrary, and, upon that supposition we ought to proceed.

19.

Having fixed upon the spot for the garden, the next thing is to *prepare the ground*. This may be done by ploughing and harrowing, until the ground, at top, be perfectly clean; and, then, by *double* ploughings: that is to say, by going, with a strong plough that turns a large furrow and turns it cleanly, twice in the same place, and thus moving the ground to the depth of fourteen or sixteen inches, for, the advantage of deeply moving the ground is very great indeed. When this has been done in one direction; it ought to be done across, and then the ground will have been well and truly moved. The ploughing ought to be done with four oxen and the plough ought to be held by a strong and careful ploughman.

20.

This is as much as I shall, probably, be able to persuade any body to do in the way of preparing the ground. But, this is not all that *ought* to be done; and it is proper to give directions for the *best* way of doing this and every thing else. The best way is, then, to *trench* the ground; which is performed in this manner. At one end of the piece of ground, intended for the garden, you make, with a spade, a trench, all along, two feet wide and two feet deep. You throw the earth out on the side away from the garden that is to be. You shovel out the bottom clean, and make the sides of the trench as nearly perpendicular as possible. Thus you have a clean open trench, running all along one end of your garden-ground. You then take another piece all along, two feet wide, and put the earth that this new piece contains into the trench, taking off the top of the new two feet wide, and turning that top down into the bottom of the trench, and then taking the remainder of the earth of the new two feet, and placing it on the top of the earth just turned into the bottom of the trench. Thus, when you have again shovelled out the bottom, and put it on the top of the whole that you have put into the trench, you have another clean trench two feet wide and two deep. You thus proceed, till the whole of your garden-ground be trenched; and then it will have been *cleanly turned over to the depth of two feet.*

21.

As to the expense of this preparatory operation, a man that knows how to use a spade, will trench four rod in a day very easily in the month of October, or in the month of November if the ground be not frozen. Supposing the garden to contain *an acre,* and the labourer to earn a dollar a day, the cost of this operation will, of course, be *forty dollars;* which, perhaps, would be twenty dollars above the expense of the various ploughings and harrowings, necessary in the other way; but, the difference in the *value* of the two operations is beyond all calculation. There is no point of greater importance than this. Poor ground deeply moved is preferable, in many cases, to rich ground with shallow tillage; and when the ground has been deeply moved *once,* it feels the benefit for ever after. A garden is made to last for *ages;* what, then, in such a case, is the amount of twenty dollars? It is well known to all who have had experience on the subject, that of two plants of almost any kind that stand for the space of three months in top soil of the same quality, one being on ground deeply moved, and the other on ground moved no deeper than is usual, the former will exceed the latter one half in bulk. And, as to *trees* of all descriptions, from the pear-tree down to the currant-bush, the difference is so great, that there is room for no comparison. It is a notion with some persons, that it is of no use to move the ground deeper than the roots of the plant penetrate. But, in the first place, the roots go much deeper than we generally suppose. When we *pull up* a cabbage, for instance, we *see* no roots more than a foot long; but, if we were carefully to pursue the roots to their utmost point, even as far as our eye would assist us, we should find the roots a great deal longer, and the *extremities* of the roots are much too fine to be seen by the *naked eye.* Upon pulling up a common turnip, who would imagine, that the side, or horizontal roots, extend to *several feet?* Yet I have traced them to the length of four feet; and Mr. Tull proved, that they extended to *six feet,* though he could not see them to that extent with his naked eye. But, though the roots should not extend nearly to the bottom of the moved ground, the plants are affected by the unmoved ground being near at hand. If this were not the case, plants with very short roots might be cultivated on a brick pavement with earth laid upon it to the thickness of a foot; and yet, no plant will live and thrive in such a state, while it will do very well in ground along side the pavement, though moved only a foot deep. Plants require a communication with, and an assistance from, beneath as well as from above, in order to give them vigour and fecundity. Plants will *live,* and will *grow* to a certain extent in earthen *pots,* or in *boxes* made of wood; but, there must be *holes in the bottom of both,* or the plants will die. See paragraphs 107 and 109.

22.

It is, therefore, of the greatest importance, that the ground be moved to a good depth, and, he who is about to make a garden should remember, that he is about to do that, the effects of which are to be felt *for ages.* There is, however, one objection to trenching in certain cases. The soil may not only not be *good* to the depth of two feet, but it may be *bad* long before you come to that depth; and, in this case, the trenching, in putting the good soil at bottom, might bring a hungry sand, or even a gravel or clay to the top, which must not be done by any means; for, even in the case of trees, they would perish, or become stunted, because their roots would not find their way from the bad soil to the good. In such cases the top soil must, in the trenching, be *kept at the top;* and, in order to effect this, your mode of proceeding, in the trenching, must be somewhat different from that described in paragraph 20.

23.

Your *first trench* must be opened in the manner described in that paragraph; but you must not then proceed to turn the *top* of the next two feet into the *bottom* of the trench. Let us suppose, now, that you have your first trench, two feet wide as before directed, open and clean. This being the case, take a foot deep of the next two feet all the way along, and, *for this once,* throw it *over the open trench* to add to the earth that you have already thrown out of that trench. Then you will have the *bottom foot* of earth left. Dig out this and turn it into the bottom of your open trench, and then the first trench will be half filled up, and you will have got your second trench open. Then go to a *new* two feet wide, that is the *third* two feet. Take the top foot deep off from this, and throw it on the *top of the* earth that you have just turned into the first trench; and then, where that first trench was there will be earth two feet deep; the bad soil at bottom and the good soil at top. Then you go on regularly. The bottom foot of the fourth two feet wide piece you turn into the bottom of the second trench, and the top foot of the third two feet wide piece you throw on the top of the earth which is at the bottom of the second trench. And, thus, when you have done, you will have moved all your ground two feet deep, and will have the bad soil at bottom and the good at top.

24.

At the *end* of your work, you will, of course, have *an open trench* and a half; and this must be filled up by carrying the earth, which came out of the first trench, round in a cart or wheel-barrow, and putting it into the space that you will have open at last. For *trees* and *asparagus,* you ought to do still *more.* See *Asparagus* in Chapter IV.

25.

It must be observed, however, that, though the soil be good in its *nature* down to two feet deep, that which comes to the top in the first mode of trenching, will not be, *immediately,* so good for *use,* as the soil which has been at top for ages. It is, in such a case, of great advantage to place the old top soil at the bottom; because when roots find the soil good to such a depth, the plants and trees thrive and bear surprizingly. But, then, the new top soil must be exceedingly well *worked* and well and judiciously manured, in order to make it equal to the old top soil: which object is, however, very soon accomplished, if the proper means be made use of.

26.

The ground being trenched, in October, ought to be well manured *at top* with good *well-rotted* dung, or with *soap-boiler's ashes,* or some other *good manure;* and this might be ploughed, or dug in shallowly. Before the frost is gone in the spring, another good coat of manure should be put on; *well-rotted* manure from the yard; ashes; or, rather, if ready, from a good *compost*. Then, when the frost is gone, the ground will be instantly fit for digging and planting; and, it will bear almost anything that can be put into it.

27.

Thus will the *ground be prepared;* and here I close my directions with regard to the nature and preparation of the soil. But, it seems necessary to add a few words on the subject of *manures* as adapted to a garden. It is generally thought, and, I believe, truly, that *dung,* of any sort, is not what ought to be used in the raising of garden vegetables. It is very certain, that they are *coarse* and *gross* when produced with aid of that sort of manure, compared to what they are when raised with the aid of *ashes, lime, rags,* and *composts.* And, besides, dung, in hot soils and hot climates, adds to the heat; while ashes, lime, rags and composts do not; but, on the contrary, they attract, and cause the earth to retain, moisture.

28.

All the ground in a garden ought *always* to be good; and it will be kept in this state if it be well manured *once every year.* Perhaps it will scarcely ever be convenient to any one to manure the whole garden at one time: and this is not of so much importance. Clay, or any earth, *burnt,* is excellent manure for a garden. It has no seeds of *weeds* or *grass* in it. A compost, made of such ashes, some wood-ashes, a small portion of horse-dung, rotten leaves, and mould shovelled up under trees, round buildings, or on the sides of roads. All these together, put into a heap, and turned over several times, make the best manure for a garden.

29.

A great deal more is done by the *fermentation* of manures than people generally imagine. In the month of June take twenty cart-loads of earth, which has been shovelled off the surface of a grassy lane, or by a road side, or round about barns, stables, and the like. Lay these twenty loads about a foot thick on some convenient spot. Go and cut up twenty good cart-loads of *weeds* of any sort, and lay these *well shaken up,* on the earth. Then cover the weeds with twenty more cart-loads of earth like the former, throwing the earth on lightly. In three days you will see the heap smoke as if on fire. If you put your hand into the earth, you will find it too hot to be endured. In a few days the heat will decline, and you will perceive the heap sink. Let it remain a week after this, and then *turn* it very carefully. This will mix the whole well together. You will find the weeds and grass in a *putrid* state. Another heating will take place, but less furious than the former. Turn it a second time in seven days: and a third time in seven days more. And by this time you will have *forty cart-loads* of manure, equal in *strength* to twenty of yard dung, and a vast deal better for a garden, or, indeed, for any other land. It is not expensive to obtain this sort of manure; and such a heap, or part of such a heap, might at all times be ready for the use of the garden. When such a heap were once formed, some ashes, fish-shells or bones reduced to powder, or other enlivening matter, might be added to it, and mixed well with it; and thus would a store be always at hand for any part of the garden that might want it.

FENCING.
30.

Here, as in the case of *Situation,* I am supposing the garden about to be *made.* Those who already have gardens, have fences. They may improve them, indeed, upon my plan; but, I am supposing the case of *a new garden;* and, I am also supposing a garden to be made in what I deem *perfection.* Those who cannot, from whatever circumstance, attain to this perfection, may, nevertheless, profit from these instructions as far as circumstances will allow.

31.

The *fence* of a garden is an important matter; for, we have to view it not only as giving *protection* against intruders, two-legged as well as four-legged, but as affording *shelter* in cold weather and *shade* in hot, in both which respects a fence may be made of great utility in an American Garden, where cold and heat are experienced in an extreme degree.

32.

In England the kitchen-gardens of gentlemen are enclosed with *walls* from ten to sixteen feet high; but this, though it is useful; and indeed necessary, in the way of protection against two-legged intruders, is intended chiefly to afford the means of raising the fruit of *Peaches, Nectarines, Apricots,* and *Vines,* which cannot, in England, be brought to perfection without walls to train them against; for, though the trees will all grow very well, and though a small sort of Apricots will sometimes ripen their fruit away from a wall, these fruits cannot, to any extent, be obtained, in England, nor the Peaches and Nectarines, even in France, north of the middle of that country, without the aid of walls. Hence, in England, Peaches, Nectarines, Apricots, and Grapes, are called *Wall-Fruit.* Cherries, Plums, and Pears, are also very frequently placed against walls; and they are always the finer for it; but, a wall is indispensably necessary to the four former.

33.

In America a fence is not wanted for this purpose; but it is very necessary for *protection;* for *shelter;* and for *shade.* As to the first, gardeners may scold as long as they please, and law-makers may enact as long as they please, mankind never will look upon taking fruit in an orchard or a garden as *felony* nor even as *trespass.* Besides, there are, in all countries, such things as *boys;* and every man remembers, if he be not very forgetful, that he himself was once a boy. So that, if you have a mind to have for your own use what you grow in your garden, the only effectual security is an insurmountable fence. This prevents the existence of *temptation,* in all cases dangerous, and particularly in that of forbidden fruit: therefore the matter reduces itself to this very simple alternative; share the produce of your garden good-humouredly with the boys of the whole neighbourhood; or, keep it for your own use by a fence which they cannot get through, under, or over. Such a fence, however it is no trifling matter to make. It must be pretty high; and must present some formidable obstacles besides its height.

34.

With regard to the second point; the *shelter,* this is of great consequence; for, it is very well known, that, on the south side of a good high fence, you can have peas, lettuces, radish, and many other things, full ten days earlier in the spring, than you can have them in the unsheltered ground. Indeed, this is a capital consideration; for you have, by this means, ten days more of spring than you could have without it.

35.

The *shade,* during the summer, is also valuable. Peas will thrive in the shade long after they will no longer produce in the sun. Currant trees and Gooseberry trees will not do well in this climate unless they be in the shade. Raspberries also are best in the shade; and, during the heat of summer, lettuces, radishes, and many other things, thrive best in the shade.

36.

It will be seen presently, when I come to speak of the *form* of a garden, that I have fixed on an *Oblong Square,* twice as long as it is wide. This gives me a long fence on the North side and also on the South side. The form gives me a fine, warm extensive border in the spring, and the latter a border equally extensive and as cool as I can get it, in the heat of summer. Of the various benefits of this shelter and this shade I shall, of course, speak fully, when I come to treat of the cultivation of the several plants. At present I shall confine myself to the *sort* of fence that I would recommend.

37.

I am aware of the difficulty of overcoming *long habit*, and of introducing any thing that is *new*. Yet, amongst a sensible people, such as those, for whose use this work is intended, one need not be afraid of ultimate success; and I, above all men, ought not to entertain such fear, after what I have seen with regard to the *Ruta Baga*. The people of this country listen patiently; and if they be not in haste to decide, they generally decide wisely at last. Besides, it is obvious to every one, that the lands, in the populous parts of the country, must be provided with a different sort of fence from that which is now in use; or, that they must be, in a few years, suffered to lay waste.

38.

Yet, with all these circumstances in my favour, I proceed with faultering accent to propose, even for a garden, a *live fence,* especially when I have to notice, that I know not how to get the plants, unless I, in the outset, bring them, or their seeds, *from England*! However, I must suppose this difficulty surmounted; then proceed to describe this fence that I would have, if I could.

39.

In England it is called a *Quick-Set Hedge.* The truth is, however, that it ought rather to be called an *Everlasting Hedge;* for, it is not, as will be seen by-and-by, so *very quickly set;* or, at least, so very quickly raised. If I could carry my readers into Surrey, in England, and *show* them quick-set hedges, I might stop here, and only provide the seeds or plants. But, not being able to do that, I must, as well as I can, describe the thing on paper. The plants are those of the *White Thorn*. This thorn will, if it be left to grow singly, attain the bulk and height of an apple-tree. It bears white flowers in great abundance, of a very fragrant smell, which are succeeded by a little berry, which, when it is ripe in the fall, is of a *red colour*. Within the red pulp is a small stone: and this stone, being put in the ground, produces a plant, or tree, in the same manner that a cherry-stone does. The red berries are called *haws;* whence this thorn is sometimes called the *haw-thorn;* as in GOLDSMITH'S Deserted Village: "The haw-thorn bush, with seats beneath the shade." The leaf is precisely like the Gooseberry leaf, only a little smaller; the branches are every where armed with *sharp thorns;* and the wood is very flexible and very tough.

40.

The haws are sown in drills, like peas, and they are taken from that situation and planted very thick in rows, in a nursery, where they stand a year or two, if not wanted the first year. Then they are ready to be planted to become a hedge. In England there are two ways of planting a hedge, as to position of ground. One on a *bank,* with a ditch on the side: the other on the *level ground.* The latter is that, of which I have now to speak.

41.

The ground for the Garden being prepared, in the manner before described under the head of *Soil,* you take up your quick-set plants, prune their roots to within four inches of the part that was at the top of the ground; or, in other words, leave the root but four inches long, taking care to *cut away all the fibres,* for they always die; and they do harm if they be left. Make the ground very fine and nice all round the edges of the piece intended for the garden. Work it well with a spade and make it very fine, which will demand but very little labour. Then place *a line along very truly;* for, mind, you are planting for generations to come! Take the spade, put the edge of it against the line; drive it down eight or ten inches deep; pull the eye of the spade towards you, and thus you make, all along a little open cut to receive the roots of the plants, which you will then put into the cut, *very upright*, and then put the earth against them with your hand, taking care not to plant them *deeper* in the ground than they stood before you took them up from the nursery. The distance between each plant is *twelve inches*. When this line is done, plant another line all the way along by the side of it, and at *six inches from it*, in exactly the same manner: but, mind, in this second line, the plants are not to stand *opposite* the plants in the first line, but opposite the *middles of the intervals*. When both lines are planted, *tread* gently between them and also on the outsides of them, and then *hoe* the ground a little, and leave it nice and neat.

42.

This work should be done in the *first* or *second week of October*, even though the leaves should yet be on the plants. For, their roots will strike in this fine month, and the plants will be ready to start off in the spring in a vigorous manner. If you cannot do it in the fall, do it the moment the ground is fit in the spring; because, if you delay it too long, the heat and drought comes, and the plants cannot thrive so well.

43.

In both cases the plants must be *cut down almost close to the ground*. If you plant in the fall, cut them down as soon as the frost is out of the ground in the spring, and *before the buds begin to swell;* and, if you plant in the spring, cut down as soon as you have planted. This operation is of *indispensable necessity;* for, without it you will have no hedge. This cutting down to within half an inch of the ground will cause the plants to send out shoots that will, in good ground, mount up to the length of three or four feet, during the summer. But, you must keep the ground between them and all about them *very clean and frequently hoed;* for the quick-sets love good culture as well as other plants.

44.

Some people cut down again the *next spring;* but, this is not the best way. Let the plants stand two summers and three winters, and cut them all *close* down to the ground as you can in the spring, and the shoots will come out so thick and so strong, that you need never cut down any more.

45.

But, you must, this year, begin to *clip.* At Midsummer, or rather, about the middle of July, you must clip off the top a little and the sides near the top, leaving the bottom not much clipped; so that the side of the hedge may *slope* like the side of a *pyramid.* The hedge will shoot again immediately, and will have shoots six inches long, perhaps, by October. Then, before winter, you must clip it again, leaving some part of the new shoots, that is to say, not cutting down to your last cut, but keeping the side always in a pyramidical slope, so that the hedge may always be wide at bottom and sharp at the top. And thus the hedge will go on getting higher and higher, and wider and wider and wider, till you have it at the height and thickness that you wish; and when it arrives at that point, there you may keep it. *Ten feet high, and five feet through at bottom,* is what I should choose; because then I have *fence, shelter* and *shade;* but, in the way of *fence,* five feet high will keep the boldest boy off from trees loaded with fine ripe peaches, or from a patch of ripe water-melons; and, if it will do *that,* nothing further need be said upon the subject! The *height* is not great; but, unless the assailant have wings, he must be content with feasting his eyes; for, if he attempt to *climb* the hedge, his hands and arms and legs are full of thorns in a moment; and he retreats as the fox did from the grapes, only with pain of body in addition to that of a disappointed longing. I really feel some remorse in thus plotting against the poor fellows; but, the worst of it is, they will not be content with fair play: they will have the *earliest* in the season, and the *best* as long as the season lasts; and, therefore, I must, however reluctantly, shut them out altogether.

46.

A hedge five clear feet high may be got in *six years* from the day of planting. And, now let us see what it has cost to get this fence round my proposed garden, which, as will be seen under the next head, is to be 300 feet long and 150 feet wide, and which is, of course, to have 900 feet length of hedge. The plants are to be a foot apart in the line, and there are to be two lines; consequently, there will be required 1800 plants, or suppose it to be *two thousand*. I think it will be strange indeed, if those plants cannot be raised and sold, at two years old, for *two dollars a thousand*. I mean *fine stout* plants; for, if your plants be poor, little slender things that have never been transplanted, but just pulled up out of the spot where they were sown, your hedge will be a year longer before it come to a fence, and will never, without extraordinary care, be so good a hedge; for, the plants ought all to be as nearly as possible of *equal size;* else some get the start of others, subdue them, and keep them down, and this makes an uneven hedge, with weak parts in it. And, when the plants are first pulled up out of the seed-bed, they are too small to enable you clearly to ascertain this *inequality of size*. When the plants are taken out of the seed-bed and transplanted into a *nursery,* they are *assorted* by the nursery men, who are used to the business. The strong ones are transplanted into one place, and the weak ones into another: so that, when they come to be used for a hedge, they are already equalized. If you can get plants *three years old* they are still better. They will make a complete hedge *sooner;* but, if they be two years old, have been transplanted, and, are at the bottom, as big as *a large goose quill,* they are every thing that is required.

47.

The cost of the plants is, then, *four dollars*. The pruning of the roots and the planting is done, in England, for about *three half pence a rod;* that is to say, about *three cents*. Let us allow *twelve cents* here. I think I could earn two dollars a day at this work; but, let us allow enough. In 900 feet there are 54 rod and a few feet over: and, therefore, the planting of the hedge would cost about *seven dollars*. To keep it clean from weeds would require about two days work in a year for five or six years: *twelve dollars more*. To do the necessary clipping during the same time, would require about *thirty dollars*, if it were done in an extraordinary good manner, and with a pair of *Garden Shears*. So that the expenses to get a complete hedge round the garden would be as follows:

	D.	C.
Plants	4	00
Planting	7	00
Cultivation	12	00
Clipping	30	00
Total	53	00

48.

And thus are a *fence, shelter* and *shade,* of everlasting duration, for a garden, containing an acre of land, to be obtained for this trifling sum! Of the *beauty* of such a hedge it is impossible for any one, who has not seen it, to form an idea: contrasted with a wooden, or even a brick fence, it is like the land of Canaan compared with the deserts of Arabia. The leaf is beautiful in hue as well as in shape. It is one of the very earliest in the spring. It preserves its bright green during the summer heats. The branches grow so thick and present thorns so numerous, and those so sharp, as to make the fence wholly impenetrable. The *shelter* it gives in the early part of spring, and the *shade* it gives (on the other side of the garden) in the heat of summer, are so much more effectual than those given by wood or brick or stone fences, that there is no comparison between them. The *Primrose* and the *Violet*, which are the earliest of all the flowers of the fields in England, always make their first appearance under the wings of the Haw-Thorn. Goldsmith, in describing female innocence and simplicity, says: "Sweet as Primrose peeps beneath the Thorn." This Haw-Thorn is the favourite plant of England: it is seen as a flowering shrub in all gentlemen's pleasure-grounds; it is the constant ornament of paddocks and parks; the first appearance of its blossoms is hailed by old and young as the sign of pleasant weather; its branches of flowers are emphatically called "May," because, according to the Old Style, its time of blooming was about the first of May, which, in England is called "May-Day;" in short, take away the Haw-Thorn, and you take away the greatest beauty of the English fields and gardens, and not a small one from English rural poetry.

49.

And why should America not possess this most beautiful and useful plant? She has English gew-gaws, English Play-Actors, English Cards and English Dice and Billiards; English fooleries and English vices enough in all conscience; and why not English *Hedges*, instead of post-and-rail and board fences? If, instead of these steril-looking and cheerless enclosures the gardens and meadows and fields, in the neighbourhood of New York and other cities and towns, were divided by quick-set hedges, what a difference would the alteration make in the look, and in the real *value* too, of those gardens, meadows and fields!

50.

It may be said, perhaps, that, after you have got your hedge to the desired height, it must still be *kept clipped* twice in the summer; and that, therefore, if the fence is *everlasting*, the trouble of it is also everlasting. But, in the first place, you can have nothing *good* from the earth without annual care. In the next place, a wooden fence will soon want nailing and patching annually, during the years of its comparatively short duration. And, lastly, what is the annual expense of clipping, when you have got your hedge to its proper height and width, and when the work may be done with a *long-handled hook* instead of a pair of *shears,* which is necessary at first? In England such work is done for a *penny a rod, twice* in the summer. Allow three times as much in America, and then the annual expense of the garden hedge will be less than *four dollars a year.*

51.

Thus, then, at the end of the *first twenty years,* the hedge would have cost *a hundred and nine dollars.* And, for ever after, it would cost only *eighty dollars in twenty years.* Now, can a *neat boarded fence,* if only eight feet high, and to *last twenty years,* be put up for less that *six dollars a rod*? I am convinced that it cannot; and, then, here is an expense for every twenty years, of *three hundred and forty-eight dollars.* A *Locust* fence, I allow, will last *for ever;* but, then, what will a fence *all of Locust, cost*? Besides the difference in the *look* of the thing; besides the vast difference in the nature and effect of the *shelter* and the *shade;* and besides, that, after all, you have, in the wooden fence, no effectual protection against *invaders.*

52.

However, there is one thing, which must not be omitted; and that is, that the hedge will not be a *fence,* or, at least, I would not look upon it as such, until it had been planted *six years.* During these six years, there must be a fence all round on the outside of it, to keep off pigs, sheep and cattle: for, as to the two-legged assailants nothing will keep them off except a quick-set hedge. If I had to make this *temporary fence,* it should be a *dead hedge,* made of split hickory rods, like those that hoops are made of, and with stakes of the stoutest parts of the same rods, or of oak saplings, or some such things. The *workmanship* of this, if I had a Hampshire or Sussex hedger, would not cost me more than six cents a rod: perhaps, the stuff would not cost more than a quarter of a dollar a rod; and this fence would last, with a little mending, as long as I should want it. But, as few good hedgers come from England, and as those who do come appear to think, that they have done enough of hedging in their own country, or, if they be set to hedging here, seem to look upon themselves as a sort of *conjurors,* and to expect to be paid and treated accordingly, the best way, probably, is, to put up a temporary post-and-rail fence, sufficient to keep out a sucking pig: and to keep this fence standing until the hedge has arrived at the age of six years, as before mentioned.

53.

There yet remains one advantage, and that not a small one, that a quick-set hedge possesses over every other sort of fence; and that is, that it effectually keeps out *poultry,* the depredations of which, in a nice garden, are so intolerable, that it frequently becomes a question, whether the garden shall be abandoned, or the poultry destroyed. Fowls seldom, or never, fly *over* a fence. They, from motives of prudence, first alight *upon it,* and then drop down on the other side; or, if they perceive danger, turn short about, and drop back again, making a noise expressive of their disappointment. Now, Fowls will alight on wooden, brick, or stone fences; but *never on a quick-set hedge,* which affords no steady lodgment for their feet, and which wounds their legs and thighs and bodies with its thorns.

54.

What has been said here of forming a hedge applies to meadows and fields as well as to gardens; observing, however, that, in all cases, the ground ought to be well prepared, and cattle, sheep and pigs kept effectually off, until the hedge arrive at its sixth year.

55.

If I am asked how the white thorn plants are to be had *in America,* I answer, that I saw a Tree of Hawthorn at *McAllister's Tavern,* near Harrisburg, in Pennsylvania, *loaded with red berries.* In short, one large tree, or bush, would soon stock the whole country; and they may be brought from England, either in plant or in berry. But, there are many here already. If more are wanted, they can be had any month of December, being shipped from England, in barrels, *half sand and half berries* in November. The berries, which are called *haws* are ripe in November. They are beaten down from the tree, and cleared from leaves and bits of wood. Then they are mixed with sand, or earth, four bushels of sand, or of earth, to a bushel of haws. They are thus put into a cellar, or other *cool* place; and here they remain, always about as moist as common earth, until *sixteen months* after they are put in; that is to say, through a *winter,* a *summer,* and *another winter;* and then they are sown (in America) as soon as the frost is clean out of the ground. They ought to be sown in little *drills;* the drills a foot a part, and the haws about as thick as peas in the drills. Here they come up; and, when they have stood 'till the next year, you proceed with them in the manner pointed out in paragraph 40.

56.

These haws may be had from *Liverpool,* from *London,* or from almost any port in Great Britain or Ireland. But, they can be had only in the months of November and December. Seldom in the latter; for, the birds eat them at a very early period. They are ripe early in November; and, *half haws half sand,* may be had, I dare say, for *two dollars a barrel,* at any place. *Three barrels* would *fence a farm*! And, as America owes to Europe her *Wheat,* why be ashamed to add *fences* to the debt? But (and with this I conclude,) if there be a resolution formed to throw all lands to common, rather than take the trifling trouble to make live fences, I do hope that my good neighbours will not ascribe these remarks to any disposition in me to call in question the wisdom of that resolution. *Figure* I, in *Plate* IV. exhibits a piece of the Garden-Hedge in elevation, in the winter season. See this Plate IV. in Chapter V.

LAYING-OUT.
57.

The *Laying-out* of a Garden consists in the division of it into several parts, and in the allotting of those several parts to the several purposes for which a garden is made. These parts consist of *Walks, Paths, Plats, Borders* and a *Hot-Bed Ground.*

58.

To render my directions more clear as well as more brief, I have given a *plan* of my proposed garden, PLATE I. This is not, strictly speaking, a plan; because it exhibits *trees* in elevation; but it will answer the purpose. Of the *sorts* of which these trees are, and of other circumstances belonging to them, I shall speak fully under the head of *Fruits.* The precise description of the *Hot-Beds* will be found under that head. At present my object is to explain the mode of Laying-out the Ground.

59.

The length of the Garden is 100 yards, the breadth 50 yards, and the area contains a statute acre; that is, 160 Rods of 16 feet to the Rod. In order to bring my length and breadth within round *numbers,* I have been obliged to add 6 rod and 58 square feet; but, with this trifling addition here is a spot containing an acre of land. Before, however, I proceed further, let me give my reasons for choosing an *Oblong Square,* instead of a *Square of equal sides.* It will be seen, that the *length* of my garden is from East to West. By leaving a greater length in this direction than from North to South, three important

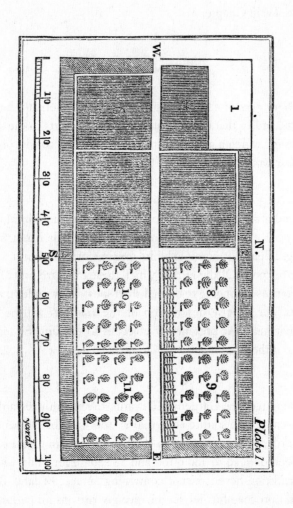

Plate 1.

advantages are secured. *First,* we get a *long* and *warm* border under the *North fence* for the rearing of things early in the spring. *Second,* we get a *long* and *cool* border under the *South* fence for *shading,* during the great heats, things, to which a burning sun is injurious. *Third,* by this shape of the area of the Garden a larger portion of the whole is sheltered, during winter and spring, from the bleak winds.

60.

Having such a spot before us, little difficulty can arise in *Laying it out.* Indeed, it is only necessary to state the *dimensions.* The several parts are distinguished by *numbers.* The long walk, running from East to West, is 6 feet wide, as is also the cross walk, in the middle. All the paths are 3 feet wide. The borders, Nos. 2 and 3, are 9 feet wide. The dimensions of the Plats Nos. 5, 7, 8, 9, 10, and 11, are (each) 70 feet from East to West and 56 from North to South. Plat, No. 6, is 56 feet by 50. Plat, No. 4, is 60 feet by 36. The Hot-bed Ground, No. 1, is 70 feet by 36. I leave trifling fractions unnoticed. In the English gardening books, they call those parts of the garden *"Quarters,"* which I call *Plats;* but, for what *reason* they so call them it would be difficult to conjecture. I call them *plats,* which is the proper word, and a word, too, universally understood. A *plat* is a piece of ground: and it implies, that the piece is *small,* compared with other larger portions, such as *fields, lots,* and the like. I will just anticipate here, that when *beds* for asparagus, onions, and other things, are made, they should run *across* the plats from North to South; and that rows of Corn, Peas, and Beans, and other *larger things* in rows, should have the same direction. But, when *beds* are sown with smaller things, the rows of those things must go *across the beds;* as will be seen when we come to speak of sowing.

61.

As to the *art* of Laying-out, it would be to insult the understanding of an American Farmer to suppose him to stand in need of any instructions. A *chain,* or a *line,* and *pole,* are all he can want for the purpose, and those he has always at hand. To form the walks and paths, is, in fact, to lay out the Garden; but, the walks and paths must be made not only *visible,* but must be *dug out.* The way is to take out the earth about four inches deep, and spread it over the adjoining ground, some on each side of the walk or path, taking care to fling, or carry, the earth, so dug out, to such a distance, that every part of the ground, which is not walk or path, receive an equal proportion of what is thus dug out. *Gravel* may be put in the walks and paths: it makes the whole look *neater;* but, in a country where the frost is so hard in winter and the ground so dry in summer, gravel can hardly be said to be *necessary,* while it may be troublesome; for, in spite of all you can do, a part of it will get into the borders; and, there it must do harm.

62.

It will be seen, that about a *third* part of the Garden is appropriated to *Fruit Trees.* The reason for this, and the uses of the other parts of the ground, will be fully stated in the Chapters on *Cultivation.* I have here treated merely of the form and the dimensions, and of the division, of the Garden. It is in treating of the cultivation of the several sorts of plants that our attention will be brought back to a close contemplation of the several parts included in this division.

II

On the Making and Managing of Hot-Beds and Green-Houses.

HOT-BEDS.

63.

I am not about to lay down rules for persons who can afford to have *cucumbers in March*. This amounts to something little short of *folly* in England: in America, it would be something worse. But, *Hot-Beds*, as things of *real use*, are more necessary in America than in England; because in the former country, the winter will not suffer to exist in the open air many plants, which are wanted to start with the warm sun, and which plants the winter *will* suffer to exist in the open air in England. The American *Spring* bears no resemblance to that of England, which comes on by degrees from the end of February to the beginning of June; while the American Spring cannot be said to be of a fortnight's duration. There is, in fact, no Spring: there is a Winter, a Summer and an Autumn, but no Spring; and none would ever have been thought of, if the *word* had not come from Europe along with many others equally inapplicable.

64.

This sudden transition from a winter, which not only puts a total stop to, but effaces all traces of, vegetation, to a summer, which, in an instant, creates swarms of insects, or warms them into life, sets the sap in rapid motion, and, in six days, turns a brown rye-field into a sheet of the gayest verdure; this sudden transition presents the gardener, or the farmer, with ground well chastened by the frost, smoking with fermentation, and with a sun ready to push forward every *plant;* but, alas! he has *no plants*! I know, that there *are persons,* who do preserve lettuce, cabbage, and other plants, during the winter, and that there *are persons,* who rear them on *Hot-beds* in the Spring; but, what I aim at, is, to render the work easy to *farmers* in particular; not only as the means of supplying their *tables,* but the stalls of their cattle, and the yards of their sheep and pigs. In the summer (a cruelly dry one) of 1819, who, within many miles of my house in Long Island, had a *loaved cabbage,* except myself? During June, July and August, I allowed *fifteen a day* for my own family: I gave *ten a day* to one neighbour; to others I gave about *five hundred,* perhaps, first and last; and, the plants were all raised in *one single light, four feet by three and a half,* on a hot-bed, made on *the* 19*th of March.* The hot-bed had six lights altogether, and was about twenty feet long; but, the part appropriated to these cabbages was only four feet by three and a half. The plants came out of this bed on the 20*th of April* and were planted three inches apart on another bed, without glass, but covered at night with a cloth. On the 20*th of May,* they were planted out in the open ground; and, on the 17*th of June* we began to eat them. All these cabbages, *Early Dwarfs, Early Yorks, Sugar Loaves,* and *Battersea,* (coming in one sort after the other) amounting to about *four thousand* in number, stood, when planted out, upon rather less than *thirty rods of ground;* and the earliest sorts, while we were using them so liberally, were selling in New York market at from 6 to 4 pence a piece.

65.

To *preserve, during Winter,* such a number of plants, or, indeed, *any* number, however small, is a work of great difficulty, and is merely *chance*-work after all. Besides, fall-sown plants are not so good as spring-sown. They become *stunted;* and they very frequently go off *to seed,* instead of producing *loaves.* However, it is not my business to treat here of *cultivation:* I am here to speak of the *Making* and *Managing* of hot-beds. This must, of course, include a description of the *Wood* and *Glass,* when formed into *Frames* and *Lights.* But, first of all, I must treat of the making of the bed.

66.

The *materials* of which the bed is to be composed, and the manner of preparing those materials, are first to be spoken of.

67.

Dung of horses, cattle, sheep or pigs, is used to make the bed of. Either may be *made to do,* with a greater or less degree of care and trouble; but, the best possible thing is *dung from the stable,* taken away before it has been *rotted,* short and long promiscuously, but rather *long* than short. If there be a large proportion of short, it may have any *litter* added to it; any *broken* straw or hay or corn stalks, in order to make a due mixture of long and short.

68.

This choosing of the materials being a very important point, I shall, in order to make my instructions clear, *suppose a case,* and such a case as will be very clear to every American Farmer.

69.

By the month of March he has always a heap of dung, which has, from time to time, been thrown out of his stable, during the winter and fall. This is *some long* and *some short.* Let the whole of this (supposing there to be *three horses* kept) be taken; and, in addition, a pretty good wagon load of long *stained* stuff from the cow-yard, or sheep-yard. Toss it down in a heap, near where you are going to make the bed. Then begin on one side of it, and take the stuff and begin making a fresh heap of it. *Shake every fork full well to pieces,* and mix well the long with the short; and thus go on, till you have the whole in a round heap rising to a point.

70.

The second day after this heap is made it will begin to send forth *steam.* Let it remain three days in this state; that is to say, *four* clear days after the day of making the heap. Then turn the heap back again; *shaking all well to pieces,* as before, and bringing to the inside that part of the stuff which was before on the outside of the heap. Let it remain now *three* clear days after the day of turning. Then turn it again; *shaking well to pieces,* as before, and bringing again the outside stuff to the inside. When it has remained *two* clear days in this state, it is fit to make the bed with.

71.

In the making the bed you will proceed as directed below; but I must first describe the *Frame* and the *Lights.* Were I speaking to persons living in a country, where there is no such thing as a hot-bed frame, I should be obliged to enter into a detailed mechanical description. But, as Frames and Lights are to be seen in almost every considerable town in America; and, as I have known very few American Farmers, who are not able to make both with their own hands, without any help from either carpenter or glazier, it will be necessary merely for me to say, that the Frame is of the best shape when it is *eighteen inches* deep at the *back,* and *nine inches* deep at the *front.* This gives *slope enough,* and especially in a country where there is so little rainy weather. The *Frame* is the wood work, on which the *Lights,* or glass-work, are laid. There needs no more than a *good look* at a thing of this sort to know how to make it, or to order it to be made. And, as it is useless to make a hot-bed without having the Frame and the Lights ready, I shall suppose them to be prepared. I suppose a *three-light* Frame, four feet wide and nine feet long, which, of course, will make every Light *three feet wide* and *four long;* because, the long way of the Light fits, of course, the cross way of the Frame.

72.

Now, then, to the work of *making the bed.* The front of the bed is, of course, to be *full South,* so that the noon sun may come right upon the glass. The length and width of the bed must be those of the Frame. Therefore, take the Frame itself, and place it *on the spot which you mean the bed to stand on.* See that you have it rightly placed; and then, with a pointed stick, make a mark in the ground all round the outside of the Frame. Then take the Frame away. Then take some sharp-pointed straight stakes, and drive them in the ground, at *each corner* of this marked-out place for the bed, and one or two on the back and on the front side. Let these be about four feet high. They are to be your guides in building the bed; and, they ought, therefore, to be very straight, and to be placed *perfectly upright.* Each stake may be placed about an inch *further out* than the mark on the ground; for fear of having the bed too narrow; though, observe, the bed should be as nearly the same length and breadth as the Frame as it is practicable to make it.

73.

In order to *begin* the work well, it is a very good way, to put some *boards* on their *edges,* on the ground, at the ends and sides, on the in-sides of the stakes; so as to have a sort of open box to begin to make the bed in. The *eye* of a *gardener* scorns such assistance; but it is very useful to persons unused to the work.

74.

Thus, all being prepared, you begin *making the bed.* Begin taking the dung on the side of your heap nearest to the spot where you are building the bed. Keep taking up clean to the ground. Have shovel as well as fork. Take long and short fairly, and mix them well as you put them in. Shake the stuff in such a way as not to suffer any *lumps.*

Shake every straw from every other straw. Let the bed *rise in* all parts together as nearly as possible. That is to say, do not put *much* in one part at one time. *Beat* the whole down with the fork as you proceed. When you have shaken on dung to the thickness of four or five inches, *beat* all over well again; and so on, till the work be finished. But *mind:* you must be very careful to keep the *edges* of the bed *well beaten;* or else they will be more *hollow,* and will *sink more,* than the rest, and then the earth on the bed will crack in the middle. Beat them well; keep them *well up* as you proceed; beat well the *sides* of the bed, as it goes on rising. Comb the sides frequently down with the spanes of the fork. And, in short, make the sides upright, and smooth and neat as a wall. As you proceed, measure the *height* frequently; in the different parts of the bed, to see that you are keeping the height every where the same. At last, shovel and sweep up all the short earthy stuff round the bed and where your dung-heap was, and lay it very smoothly on the top of the bed; and make all as smooth and as level as a die with the back of your shovel.

75.

Thus the *bed is made.* Then put on the Frame, and fix it nicely. Then put the Lights upon the Frame. If you finish your bed by noon, the *heat will* begin to rise by the next morning; and, by the noon of the second day after the bed is made, the heat will be up. Poke your finger as deep as you can into the middle of the bed, when you have taken off one of the Lights. If the heat be so great as to *burn* your finger; that is to say, if you cannot *endure* the heat; then it is too great to receive the earth; but, if not, *put on the earth* all over the bed. If the heat be too great, give the bed a little *air,* and wait till a little of the heat be gone off.

76.

The earth should be *dry;* not like *dust;* but, not *wet.* I made provision for my bed, by putting earth in my *cellar,* in November. It is not much that is wanted. The bed is to be covered all over, about *six inches deep*. When the earth has been on twenty-four hours, take off the lights, and stir the earth well with your *hands;* for, *hands* are the only tools used in a hot-bed. When you have stirred the earth well, and made it *level* and smooth, you may *sow your seed,* if you do not find the earth too hot. But, observe, the earth is to be *level,* and *not sloping* like the glass. The glass is sloping to meet the *sun,* and to turn off the *wet;* but, the earth must lie perfectly level; and this, you will observe, is a very great point.

77.

Next comes *the act of sowing.* The more *handsomely* this is done, the *better* it is done. A handsome dress is *better* than an ugly one, not because it is warmer, or cooler, but because, liking it better, being more pleased with it, we *take more care of it.* Those who have seen two or three women together, crossing dirty streets, or in danger from horses or carriages, where the volunteer assistance of men became useful; those philosophers, who have been spectators of scenes like this, cannot have failed to discover, that humanity, like smoke, is very apt to fly to the fairest; and I much question whether Nicodemus Broadbrim himself, if he saw a pretty girl and an ugly one stuck in the mud, would not give his hand to the former. He would hand them *both* out to a certainty; but, he would extricate the pretty one *first.* There is a great deal in the *look* of our gardens and fields; and, surely, in so diminutive a concern as a hot-bed, all ought to be neat and regular. Seeds are great *telltales;* for, when they come up, we discover all the carelessness that may have prevailed at the sowing of them.

78.

When you have taken off all the lights, make little drills with your finger, from the back of the bed to the front, *half an inch deep* and about *an inch apart.* Make them equi-distant, parallel, and straight. Then drop in your *Cabbage* seeds along the drills, very thin;

but, *twenty* seeds, perhaps in an inch; for, some will not grow, and some may be pulled up when they appear. It is better to have *rather* too many than too few. When you have dropped in your seeds all over the bed, and distinguished the several sorts of Cabbages by names, or numbers, written on a bit of paper, and put into the cleft of a little stick, stuck in the ground; then cover all the seeds over neatly and smoothly. Put on the lights; and look upon your spring work as happily begun.

79.

But, now we come to the *management* of a hot-bed. And, observe, that the main principle is, *always to give as much air as the plants will endure.* I have always observed, that the great and prevalent error is, an *endeavour to obtain, by exclusion of air,* something to make up for *the want of bottom heat.* It is not thus that nature operates. She gives the *air* as well as the heat; and, without the former she gives nothing. I suppose the hot-bed, made as above, to be about *four feet high,* when just finished. It will sink as it heats; and will, at last, come to about a *foot and a half.* Its heat will gradually diminish; but, it will give a great heat for about six weeks; and *some* heat for *four* months. It is this *bottom* heat that makes things *grow.* The *sun* is often hot in May; but, it is not till the *earth* is warm that vegetation advances with rapidity.

80.

Having secured the *bottom* heat, make free with the *air.* Even before the seeds begin to appear, give air to the bed every day, unless it be *very cold weather indeed.* The usual way of giving air is by bits of thick board, cut in the shape of a triangle, or, rather, like a *wedge,* broad at one end, and coming to a point at the other. Each light is lifted up, either at back or front of the frame, as the wind may be, and the wedge, or *tilter,* as it is called, is put in, to hold the light up. But, if more air be wanted, the lights may be shoved up, or down: and, in a fine day, actually taken off.

81.

When the plants come up, they will soon tell you all about *air;* for, if they have not enough, they will *draw up* long-legged, and will have small seed leaves, and, indeed, if too much deprived of air, will drop down and die. Take care in time to prevent this. Let them grow *strong* rather than *tall. Short* stems, *broad seed leaves,* very *green;* these are the signs of good plants and proper management.

82.

It will be necessary to *water.* Take off a light at a time, and water with a watering pot that does not pour out heavily. Water just about sunset: and then shut down the lights; and the heat will then rise, and make the plants grow prodigiously.

83.

As soon as the plants are *fairly up,* thin them, leaving *four in an inch;* and stir the ground about, at the same time with your finger. This will leave in the frame from *twenty-five* to *thirty thousand plants.* If you want less, sow in wide rows and thinner in the row. But, above *all things,* give air enough. Do not attempt to make the plants *grow fast.* You are sure to destroy them, if you make this attempt. Have patience. The plants will be ready soon enough. Get them *strong* and *green;* and, to do this, you must give them *plenty of air.* Remember, that, out of a thousand failures in hot-bed culture, nine hundred and ninety-nine arise from the giving of *too little air.*

84.

Before I proceed to the time of taking the plants out of the bed, I must make a remark or two respecting *shelter* for hot-beds; and this leads me back to the *Plan of the Garden.* In that plan (*Plate* I.) is the *Hot-bed Ground,* No. 1, which is 70 feet by 36. The fence to the North and West is the *hedge,* and that to the South and East ought to be made of *Broom Corn Stalks,* in this manner: Put some Locust-Posts along at eight or ten feet apart. Let these posts be ten feet high and squared to three inches by three inches. Lay a bed of bricks, or smooth stones, along the ground from post to post, and let this bed be about seven or eight inches wide. This bed is for the bottoms of the Broom-Corn Stalks to stand on. Go on one side of the row of posts, and nail three rows of strips, or laths (best of Locust,) to the posts. The first row at a foot and a half from the ground; the second row at six feet from the ground; and third row within six inches of the top of the posts. Then do the same on the other side of the posts. Thus you will have a space of three inches wide, all the way along, between these opposite rows of strips. Then take fine, long, straight Broom-Corn Stalks, and fill up this space with them, full and tight, putting them, of course, bottoms downwards, and placing these bottoms upon the bricks. When the whole is nicely filled, strain a line from top of post to top of post, and according to that line, cut off the tops of the Broom-Corn Stalks; and, while the fence will look very handsome, it will be *a shelter* much more effectual than pales or a wall; and, in my opinion, will last as long as the former, unless the former be made wholly of Locust. Stalks, rushes, reeds, straw, twigs, bows, any thing of this kind, formed into a fence, or put up as shelter, is preferable to any thing *smooth* and *solid.* Grass will shoot earlier under a *bush,* than under a wall, or even a house. A wall will not save your ears from the sharp winds so effectually as even a thin hedge. The American farmer knows well the warmth that walls of Corn-Stalks afford.

85.

However, it is not to be presumed, that a *Hot-Bed Ground* will be made by every farmer; and, therefore, before I proceed further with my instructions about it, let me proceed upon the supposition, that the aforementioned bed is made in some *open place.* In this case it will be necessary to use some precautions as to *shelter.*

86.

While the dung is *working,* before it be made into the bed, it must, in case of *very sharp frost,* be *covered,* especially on the North and North West sides. If it be not, it will freeze on these sides, and, of course, will not ferment. However, this is no troublesome job: you have only to throw on a parcel of straw, or stalks; and take them off again, when the frost relaxes. When the bed is *made,* this is what I did. I drove some stakes down, four feet distant from the bed, opposite the North Side and the West End. I tacked a pole from stake to stake; and then I placed up along against this pole, three or four rows of sheaves of tall Corn-Stalks. This sheltered the bed from the North West winds, and prevented it from freezing on that quarter. Some sheaves might, besides, if necessary, be laid against the bed itself. But, observe, you must be able to get at the Lights constantly to give air, and to see how things go on; and, therefore, it is better to have your shelter at some feet distance from the bed.

87.

We now return to the bed and the plants. I suppose the seed to have been sown on the 10th of March (*Long Island,* mind,) and that you have been very attentive to give *air* and *water.* By the 10th of April, the plants will have *eight leaves,* and they will form one solid patch of green. They will be a little *drawn up,* though you have given them plenty of air. And now they must be removed into a new bed. Dig out the ground a foot deep, four feet wide and to as great a length as is required by your number of plants. Fill this hollow up with the best dung you have, cover it over with four inches of good earth; and plant your plants upon it in rows four inches apart, and two inches apart in the row. When you have put out the plants, water them lightly; and *shade* them for two or three days from the sun. They must also be sheltered *every night,* in this manner. Take some rods, put one end of each rod into the ground on one side of the bed, and the other end on the other side; put these rods at about two feet asunder all along the bed; then tie some rods long ways to these arched rods; so that, when you have done, your bed has an *arch* over it formed by these rods. Every evening about sun-set, cover this arch with mats, with old carpets, or with a slight covering of any sort, which take off again at sun-rise in the morning.

88.

To put out *all* your plants in this way will require a *very* long bed, or many short ones. If, therefore, your number of plants be very large, the best way will be to put out a part of them in this way, leave the remainder in the hot bed a week longer, (taking off the lights in the day time,) and then to plant all the remainder out in beds of fine rich earth, in the natural ground, and without any covering.

89.

Now here we drop, for the present, the subject of *Cabbage-Plants;* because I am to speak of their culture, under the word, *Cabbage,* in that part of the work, which will treat of the cultivation of Vegetables. I am, in this part of my work, to confine myself to the *making and managing of Hot-Beds;* and, I have selected the *Cabbage-Plant,* as a subject for explaining my meaning, because I think that the raising of that plant is one of the most useful purposes, to which a hot-bed can be applied in America.

90.

But, a Hot-Bed may be applied to many other purposes. *Lettuces* may be raised in it. Pepper-grass, Radishes, young Onions, may be raised. Parsley-roots may be put in, and fine parsley obtained in March. Asparagus may be raised in this way. It is not worth while to attempt to bring Cucumbers and Melons to *fruit* in a hot-bed: but the *plants* may be raised there, and afterwards put out in the ground with great advantage in point of *time.* Several sorts of annual *flowers* and of *Green-house* plants may be got forward by a hot-bed, which, without it, can hardly be got at all to any great degree of perfection. Of the management of these sorts of plants in a hot-bed I shall speak under their several *names;* but, on the management of hot-beds, there yet remain to be made some observations, which have a general application.

91.

As to *heat* and *air* it will demand but little attention to manage well. But, a little *Termometre,* hung up, or laid down, in the bed, will be of use. The heat should not exceed *seventy-five* degrees in the day time, and *sixty* at night. If it come down to fifty at night it is better. If you cannot keep it down to sixty without giving a little *air* at night, give it, by putting something under a light, or two lights, to let in a little of the cold. For, always bear in mind, that, when plants, of whatever kind, be *drawn up,* they are nearly spoiled.

92.

When the *Sun* comes upon the glass, it soon augments the heat; and the air must be given immediately if possible, so as to keep down the heat. Changes are very sudden in March, April, mid-May; and, therefore, *somebody* should always be at hand to attend to the hot-bed. But, if the master be from home, there is, surely, some man; or, at any rate, a wife, a son, or a daughter. The labour is nothing, the trouble very little indeed, and all that is wanted is a small portion of *care.*

93.

It may happen that the bed will get *too cool.* It may lose its heat *sooner* than you could wish, especially if you use it for Cucumber and Melon-plants after you have used it for things that you want earlier; and, I shall show, that this may be very *useful* in certain cases. Now, if the heat be too much diminished, you may easily restore it, thus: make a little narrow hot-bed, a *foot and a half wide,* all round the bed. Put the dung together as before; place it close to the bed; beat it well; and build it up, all round, as high as the *top of the Frame.* This is called *lining;* and it will give the bed nearly as much heat as it had at first. If you do not want so much heat, line only the *back* of the bed; or the back and the *two ends.* In short, take as much heat as you may want.

94.

Before I dismiss the subject of hot-beds. I must notice, that there are other contrivances than *frames* resorted to in this kind of garden work. A *frame* is, as we here see, a wooden construction, for *lights* of glass to be placed on. For smaller concerns there are very convenient things, called *hand-lights,* or *hand-glasses.* A hand-glass is a square *glass-house in miniature.* Its sides are about eight inches high from the ground to the eves. The roof rises from each side in a triangular form, so that it comes to a point at the top, as a pyramid does, the base of which is a square. At this point is a *stout ring,* to lift the hand-glass about. The panes of glass are fixed in *lead;* and the rim round the bottom is made of iron or of wood. Any glazier can make these hand-lights, and they are by no means expensive. Here, where the tax upon glass is so slight, they cannot be more expensive than in England; and there they do not cost much more than a dollar each. They may be made of almost any size. About 18 inches square at the base is a very good size. In the gardens near London there are acres of ground covered with such glasses. It is the custom there to plant out cauliflowers in the fall, and to cover them, in severe weather, during winter, with hand-glasses. A hand-glass may, in April, be put over a hot-bed made with a *wheel-barrow full of dung.* It would bring on cabbage plants enough for two or three *gardens.* It is handy to sow things under in the *natural ground,* in the spring, especially flowers that are to be transplanted; for, on the natural ground, it adds to the heat in the day, and keeps off cold and slight frost in the night. Air is given, by putting a brick, or bit of wood, under one of the sides of the hand-glass.

95.

Now, look back at the *Plan* of the garden. No. I, is the Hot-bed Ground. It is seventy feet long and thirty-six wide. It is wide enough to contain four rows of hot-beds, with room for linings. But, though a tenth part of this should not be wanted, the place is *a warm place,* and is better for tender things than a colder place. The entrance to it from the Western door of the garden is convenient for the carrying in of dung, and for carrying it out again for the use of the garden.

96.

Here would be room for a great deal more beds, certainly, than can ever be wanted even in a gentleman's garden. But, observe, the room is no evil. Whatever is not used for hot-beds may be applied to other purposes. This is a *sheltered* spot; and, it will, by and by, be seen, that, even if not used for hot-beds at all; such a spot must be of great utility.

GREEN-HOUSES.
97.

My object is not to treat of any thing very *expensive,* or very *curious.* There are persons, whose taste greatly differs from mine in regard to shrubs and flowers; and I by no means pretend to say that mine is the best. But, I can treat of nothing that I do not *understand,* that is to say, of nothing with regard to which I have not had experience. My study, as to gardening, has always been directed towards things that please the *senses:* in vegetables, things that please the *palate,* and that, to use the common saying, are *good to eat:* in shrubs and flowers, things that delight the *sight,* or the *smell.* Mere *botanical curiosities,* as they are called, I never took delight in. If the merit of a plant or a flower is not to be discovered without close and somewhat painful examination, it has always appeared to me not worth the looking for. There is, in fact, nothing *more curious* in one plant, or flower, than in another. They are all equally curious; they are equally objects of wonder. There is more of *rareness,* in England, in the Indian Corn than in the Cowslip; but *here,* the Cowslip would have the merit of rareness. The ice-plant, the egg-plant, and many others, have *oddity* to recommend them; but, after all, *oddity* is but a poor recommendation. What are thousands of these when compared to a single *rose* bush in bloom!

98.

I am rather anticipating here; but, I wished to explain why I do not recommend any very great pains in the affair of a green-house. The *plants* to keep in such a place I will talk of hereafter. At present I am to speak of the *making* and the *managing* of such a place.

99.

A green-house is for the purpose of having plants and flowers flourishing, or, at least, in verdure and in bloom, in *winter.* The best place for a green-house, is, near the dwelling house, and, it should be actually *joined* to the dwelling house, one of the rooms of which should have *windows looking into the* green-house, which latter, however, must face the *South.* When the thing can be thus contrived, it is very pretty. It renders a long winter shorter in appearance; and, in such cases, appearances are realities. A door, opening from a parlour into a green-house, makes the thing very pleasant and especially in a country like America, where, for six months, every thing like verdure is completely absent from the fields and gardens. And, if the expense be but small, such a pleasure may, surely, be afforded to the females of a family, though, to afford it, may demand some deduction in the expenditure for the *bottle,* in the pleasures of which (if, alas! pleasures they be!) the amiable ladies of this country do not partake.

100.

I hope, that no man, who has the means to provide such pleasures for his wife, or daughters, will talk to me about the *uselessness* of a green-house. Of what *use*, then, is *fine* linen, when coarse is cheaper and will last longer? Of what *use* is beauty in a *horse*, a *house*, or in any thing else? Of what *use* are sporting dogs and guns? The *use* of these things is, that they *give pleasure;* that they render life pleasanter than it would be without them. And, why not, on the same principle, call a green-house *useful?* Of what *use* is money, that thing which every one seeks to possess? Of what use indeed, but to be expended on things, which tend to make life easy and pleasant? Therefore, a green-house comes fairly within the scope of usefulness; for, from it the females of a family would receive constant amusement and delight, during a season when they are cut off from almost all other recreation.

101.

Let me not, however, in using these arguments, be supposed to doubt of the disposition of American husbands to gratify their wives in this respect; for, many and striking as are the traits, that distinguish the American character, none is so striking, and none exalts it so much, as the respect and deference of the male towards the female sex. They talk to us about French *politeness;* and we hear enough of the sentimental trash of romances, where Princes and Nobles are the heroes. But, in no part of this whole world are the women so kindly and so respectfully treated by the men as in America. Here women, in no state of life, are treated badly or churlishly. To insure indulgence, assistance, forbearance, from *every man,* and under any circumstances, it is sufficient that the party is *a woman.* In this respect no country on earth will bear a comparison with America. This is, too, the *natural* bent of the human heart when uncorrupted by vicious courses and unhardened by penury. For, count our real pleasures; count the things that delight us through life: and you will find, that ninety-nine out of every hundred are derived from women. To be the object of *no woman's* care or good wishes is a sentence the most severe that can be pronounced upon man.

102.

As to the *erection* of a green-house, carpenters and glaziers are never wanted, and, where Locust wood, for the sills, is every where to be had, and glass with scarcely any tax, how elegant, how cheap, and how durable, may such a thing as a green-house be!

103.

In America there must be *heat;* but, how easily will any of the ingenious men in this country find the means of furnishing the necessary heat with hardly any expense or trouble! In most cases the warmth might go from the parlour fire place; for, all that is wanted, is *completely to keep out frost.* There is, here, no want of *Sun* even in the coldest weather; and, if the green-house were on the *Eastern* side of the dwelling-house, the cold would not be any great annoyance. But, at any rate, the heat necessary to keep out frost might easily be obtained. A *Termometre* should be kept in the green-house. The heat should be about *sixty* degrees in the day time, and *forty-five* in the night.

104.

In England they need very little fire in their green-houses, except in very cold weather, which, indeed, they seldom have. Their great want is that of *sun;* for, nothing will do well without sun; and America has plenty of this even in the coldest weather. So that, if the frost were *effectually* kept out that alone would give beautiful plants in winter. By an additional heat, a *growth* and a *bloom* would be constantly kept up; and a green-house might be made one of the most beautiful and most pleasant things in the world.

105.

Of the different plants suitable for a green-house, and of the particular treatment of each, I shall speak under the head of FLOW-ERS; and shall, in this place, only add some directions as to *management,* which are applicable to the whole assemblage.

106.

Air is the main thing, after the keeping out of the frost. Air is given by pushing up, or drawing down, the *Lights,* which form the *top* or roof of the green-house. Always give air, when there is no fear of frost. Give heat and air at the same time, if the weather be not mild enough to dispense with the heat. For, without air, the plants will become sickly. They have *lungs* as well as we; and, though they may *live,* for a while, without air, they will be an eye-sore instead of a delight to the beholder. If the *sides* and *front,* as well as the *top,* of the green-house, be of glass, (which is best,) then air may be given there, instead of giving it by pushing up, or pulling down, the lights at *top.*

107.

The plants, of whatever sort or size, must be in what the English call *pots,* and what the Americans call *jars.* Perhaps I may as well speak, once for all, about the shape and size, and manner of planting in, these pots. The shape is generally well known; but, the pots ought *never to be glazed.* Plain earthen pots are best as well as cheapest. There must be a hole in the middle of the bottom of every pot, or no plant will *live* in it for any considerable length of time, and will never *grow* in it at all. This hole should be in proportion to the size of the pot; and the pots may be from 4 inches to 18 inches over at top, and from 4 inches to 18 inches deep; being one third less across at bottom than at the top. The smallest hole ought to be of the size of *half a dollar.*

108.

Besides the *pot,* there is what the English call *a pan,* for the pot to stand in, which should be about 2 inches deep, and as wide over as the *top* of the pot, and, of course, a third part wider than the bottom of the pot. This pan should be made of the same materials with the pot itself.

109.

I have, in paragraph 21, mentioned, incidentally, *wooden boxes,* as things wherein to place plants; but, I must here caution the reader against the practice, wherever it can be avoided, especially for small plants. We see plants, thus cultivated, placed on window sills; and they sometimes grow there pretty well. Orange Trees, Large Myrtles, and other large exotics, are planted in *tubs.* There would be great difficulty in getting earthen things of sufficient dimensions for these purposes; besides the constant danger of *breaking.* But, I am quite satisfied, that where earthenware can be got and used, it is greatly preferable to wood; and this opinion is founded on actual experience. In my hot-bed of 1819, I sowed several sorts of seeds in *little wooden boxes.* I had no pots at hand, and to get them from New York required more time than I was willing to spare. The seeds all *came up;* but, by the time that they were an inch or two high, they *rotted at the stem,* and fell down. They were not less than twenty sorts of seeds; some of culinary vegetables, some of field-plants, and some of forest-trees. They all died. In one box there were planted some *geranium-cuttings.* They came out into bud and leaf; but died soon afterwards. I had soon afterwards got some *pots.* I repeated my sowing and planting; all the seeds and plants *grew and flourished.* And, let it be observed, that the boxes stood in the same bed, where cabbages and cauliflowers were sown without either pots or boxes; and that the plants of these grew, and flourished exceedingly. The cause of the plants rotting in the boxes was this: though there were several holes at the bottom of each box, and though these were properly covered with oyster-shells, the wood *itself,* sides as well as bottom, *imbibed,* and *retained too long,* part of the water poured on the top, and, as the boxes were plunged into the earth of the bed, they imbibed moisture from the watering of the bed also. There was constantly *stagnant and sour water near the roots of the plants,* and this killed them. These boxes were of *deal.* If *tubs,* or *boxes,* must be resorted to, they ought to be of *Locust,* or some other *hard* and *close* wood. Locust is best, because *imperishable.* See paragraph 16.

110.

Some care is necessary in sowing and planting in pots. The mould should be good, and made very fine. The first thing is to put an *oyster shell,* or piece of broken earthen ware, into the pot, to *cover the hole at the bottom;* and the *hollow* part of the shell, or other thing, should be *downwards.* The use of this is, to keep the hole *open,* that the water may find its way out of the pot, and not lie stagnant at the bottom, where it would become sour and injure, if not kill, the plant. The earth, if there were no shell, would fill up the hole, and, would, in time, become solid, and thus prevent the water from getting out. The shell, or broken earthen ware, keeps the earth hollow, and the water creeps under the edges of it, and thus escapes into the pan, whence it evaporates. In fields, we always desire an *open under-soil;* and, in a rainy season, you will see the crops stunted and looking yellow, where there is a bottom of *clay,* while, at the very same time, a bottom of sand, gravel, lime stone, or other *open* matter, exhibits them green and flourishing. It is upon this principle, founded on experience, that holes have been made in the bottom of flower-pots. The uses of pans, are, first, to prevent the water from running about the places where pots are placed; and next to hold the water up to a level with the roots, in *hot* situations, a little longer than it would otherwise remain up to that level. See paragraph 21.

111.

As to the mere operation of sowing, or planting, things in pots, though a simple operation enough, some little attention to method is necessary. Your mould always ought to be *fine*, and even *sifted*, if convenient; for, when the quantity is to be reckoned by *gallons*, the labour cannot be great; and the desire to possess greenhouse plants necessarily implies pleasure, rather than pain, in employing the means to obtain them. In order to make myself clearly understood, I shall suppose an instance of *sowing* and one of *planting*.

112.

Suppose you have the seeds of *Stocks* to sow. Put earth into the pot enough to fill it to within an inch of the top, and make the top of the earth very *smooth*. Then scatter your seeds upon it, and not too thickly. Then crumble some earth over the seeds to the depth of about half an inch. Make the top very smooth again. Then take the pot in your two hands, and give five or six *gentle taps* with the bottom of the pot *upon the ground*, or upon *a block*, or some *solid* thing. This *settles the earth down;* and it needs no pressing at the top, nor any other thing done to it. After this settling, the top of the earth should be about an inch *lower* than the top of the pot; else you could not, when necessary, give water; for the water would run off, there being no place to hold it.

113.

Suppose you have a *Geranium* to plant, which has been raised from a cutting, and the root of which cannot be very large. Put some earth in the pot. Hold the root of the plant upon it to see that it will be of the *right depth*, if its root stand on that earth. Then, when you have got the earth to the right height, hold the plant with one hand, and fill up the pot, round the plant, with the other. Then, tap the bottom of the pot on some solid thing, as before mentioned, leaving the earth, as before, an inch *lower* than the top of the pot. Put the pot in the pan; and, in this case, *water* the plant moderately; for, observe, that a plant in a pot has not an under-soil and dews and a mass of fermenting earth to supply it with moisture, as a plant in the open air has. Yet, even in the case of pots, it is best, unless the plant be of a very juicy nature, to suffer the ground to get *dry at top before you water;* because, water falling upon *freshly-moved earth,* always makes it *bake* hard at top, which is very injurious to every kind of plant.

114.

These two instances will suffice for the operation of sowing and planting in pots; for, though some seeds and some plants will be larger, or smaller, than those here mentioned, the principle is the same, and the difference in minute particulars will point itself out. If, for instance, you have stocks, or other little things, to transplant into pots, you will nearly fill the pot with earth, and then make holes with a little stick, or with a finger, to put in the roots; and then proceed as before, and settle down the earth. Such little things, being nearly all juice, will require *water* directly, and shading for a day or two. But, about these matters I shall say more by-and-by, when I come to the *cultivation* of the several sorts of plants and flowers.

115.

The *benches* of the green house remain to be spoken of. They should rise one above another like the steps of a stairs, that the whole of the plants may share in the benefit bestowed by the sun; but, there may be some on the ground, or floor; and, indeed, the precise arrangement must be left to the taste of the owner. The arrangement ought, however, to be such as to make it convenient to get at every pot; not only for the purpose of watering, but for that of picking off the dead, or dying leaves; for that of stirring the earth frequently round the stems of the plants; and for that of sweeping, and even washing, the benches and the floor. For, let it be observed, that, besides the neatness of keeping, due to so choice and elegant a matter as a green-house, cleanliness is greatly conducive to the health of plants in a confined situation. In short, it is *beauty* that is here sought; and, *can* there be beauty without cleanliness!

116.

In the month of *June* (Long Island, observe) the plants come out of this their winter abode. How they are then to be disposed of will be treated of hereafter, under the head of flowers; where it will be seen, that the green-house, besides being a most charming object in winter, when all without is dreariness, is the best security for giving you a beautiful garden in summer; and that without a green-house, or, at least, a hot-bed, it is quite impossible to have in perfection, either in America or in England, certain plants and flowers, some of which are the very greatest beauties of the beautiful family of Flora.

117.

Nor must we forget some things, with regard to which a green-house would be of great *use*, even according to the most vulgar notions of utility. All sorts of *Herbs* might be potted, and kept green and growing in the green-house during the winter. Some Herbs *dry* well; but, none of them are quite so good as when *green*; and, as to *Parsley*, which is wanted almost every day in the year, it loses all its *virtue* in the drying, smell and all. Six large pots of parsley, the plants taken out of the ground and put in pots in September, and put into the green-house in November, will supply a large family well; and this is no trifling thing, when, for love or money, a sprig of parsley is not to be got for months. A Sage tree, a tree of Rue, one of Rosemary, one of Lavender, a root of Hyssop, Thyme, Penny-royal, some Mint, and, indeed, of every pot and medicinal Herb, that is usually grown in the garden, would be useful, as well as pleasant to the eye, during winter.

118.

Even when the plants are out of the green-house, the latter is of *use*. An excellent place for the *drying* of *cherries, apples, pears, quinces, peaches*, and other fruits; and also for the drying of *yeast-cakes*, one of the most useful articles that sensible and provident house-wives ever invented.

119.

All this work of drying *can*, indeed, be performed by the help of the fine hot sun, in the *open air*; but, then, wet days come; and, some-times, the being compelled to take the things into the house, to place them in a confined space, and in the shade, at best, and away from strong light, greatly injures, and, sometimes, spoils them; and, at any rate, they must always be taken in at *night* and put out again in the day time. All these are impediments; and all these impedi-ments would be, at once, removed by having a green-house. Once the articles were placed properly in that, the process of drying would be completed without more trouble, and in about half the time required to obtain even an imperfect operation in the open air.

120.

For these purposes, too, only on a smaller scale, a *hot-bed frame*, when done with, for raising plants for the year, would be useful. The frame and lights might be placed upon *boards*, and the fruits, or cakes, put upon these boards. Being shut in, neither rains nor dews could affect them. They would be dried quicker, more effectually, and with a tenth part of the trouble that attends the drying in the open air.

121.

Thus, then, I think, that there is *use*, even in the vulgar sense of the word, as well as ornament, in a green-house. But, I must confess, that its value, in my eyes, consists in its *moral* effects. It is a source of pleasure to the Mistress of the mansion; to her, who has so strong a claim to attention and indulgence. I will not praise pursuits like these, with LORD BACON, because, "God Almighty first *planted a garden;*" nor with COWLEY, because "a garden is *like Heaven;*" nor with ADDISON, because "a garden was the habitation of our first parents *before the fall;*" all which is rather far-fetched, and puts one in mind of the grave dispute between the *Gardeners* and *Tailors,* as to the antiquity of their respective callings; the former contending that the *planting* of the garden took place *before* the *sewing* of the fig-leaves together; and the latter contending, that there was no *gardening* at all, till Adam was expelled and compelled to *work;* but, that the *sewing* was a real and bona fide act of tailoring. This is vulgar work to be sure; it is grovelling; but, who can blame such persons, when they have LORD BACON to furnish them with a precedent?

122.

I like, a great deal better than these writers, SIR WILLIAM, who so ardently and yet so *rationally* and *unaffectedly* praises the pursuits of gardening, in which he delighted from his youth to his old age. But, I look still further, as to effects. There must be *amusements* in every family. Children observe and follow their parents in almost every thing. How much better, during a long and dreary winter, for daughters, and even sons, to assist, or attend, their mother in a green-house, than to be seated with her at *cards,* or at any other amusement that can be conceived! How much more innocent, more pleasant, more free from temptation to evil, this amusement than *any other!* How much more *instructive* too! "Bend the twig when young:" but, here, there needs no *force;* nay, not even persuasion. The thing is so pleasant in itself; it so naturally meets the wishes;

that the taste is fixed at once, and it remains, to the exclusion of cards and dice, to the end of life.

123.

This is, with me, far more than sufficient to outweigh even a plausible objection on the score of expense. Such husbands and fathers as are accessible by arguments like these, will need nothing more to induce them to yield to my recommendation with such as are not, no arguments within the reach of my capacity would be of any avail.

III

ON PROPAGATION AND CULTIVATION IN GENERAL.

124.

In order to have good Vegetables, Herbs, Fruits, and Flowers, we must be careful and diligent in the Propagation and Cultivation of the several plants; for, though nature does much, she will not do all. He, who trusts to chance for a crop, deserves none, and he generally has what he deserves.

125.

The PROPAGATION of plants is the *bringing of them forth,* or the *increasing and multiplying* of them. This is effected in several different ways: by *seed,* by *suckers,* by *offsets,* by *layers,* by *cuttings.* But, bear in mind, that *all* plants, from the Radish to the Oak, *may* be propagated by the means of *seed;* while there are many plants which can be propagated by *no other means;* and, of these, the Radish and the Oak are two. Let me just qualify, here, by observing, that I enter not into the deep question (which so many have puzzled their heads with) of *equivocal generation.* I confine myself to things of which we have a certain knowledge.

With regard to Propagation by means *other* than that of seed, I shall speak of it fully enough under the names of the several plants, which are, as to the way of propagating them, to be considered as exceptions to the general rule. Therefore, I shall, in the present Chapter, treat of propagation by *seed* only.

126.

CULTIVATION must, of course, differ in some respects, to suit itself to certain differences in the plants to be cultivated; but, there are some principles and rules, which apply to the cultivation of all plants; and it is of these only that I propose to speak in the present Chapter.

127.

It is quite useless, indeed it is grossly absurd, to prepare land, and to incur trouble and expense, without duly, and even *very carefully,* attending to the *seed* that we are going to sow. The *sort,* the *genuineness,* the *soundness,* are all matters to be attended to, if we mean to avoid mortification and loss. Therefore, the first thing is, the

SORT OF SEED.
128.

We should make *sure* here; for, what a loss to have *late* cabbages instead of *early* ones! As to beans, peas, and many other things, there cannot easily be mistake or deception. But, as to cabbages, cauliflowers, turnips, radishes, lettuces, onions, leeks, and numerous others, the eye is no guide at all. If, therefore, you do not *save your own seed,* (of the manner of doing which I shall speak by and by,) you ought to be very careful as to whom you purchase of; and, though the seller be a person of perfect probity, he may be deceived himself. If you do not save your own seed, which, as will be seen, cannot always be done with safety, all you can do, is, to take every precaution in your power when you purchase. Be very particular, very full and clear, in the order you give for seed. Know the seedsman well, if possible. Speak to him yourself, on the subject, if you can; and, in short, take every precaution in your power, in order to avoid the mortifications like those of having one sort of cabbage, when you expected another, and of having rape when you expected turnips or ruta-baga.

TRUE SEED.
129.

But, besides the *kind*, there is the *genuineness* to be considered. For instance, you want *sugar-loaf cabbage*. The seed you sow may be *cabbage*: it may, too, be *sugar-loaf*, or more that than any thing else: but, still, it may not be *true to its kind*. It may have become degenerate; it may have become *mixed*, or *crossed*, in generating. And thus, the plants may very much disappoint you. *True* seed is a great thing: for, not only the time of the crop coming in, but the quantity and quality of it, greatly depend upon the *trueness* of the seed. You have *plants*, to be sure; that is to say, you have *something* grow; but you will not, if the seed be not *true*, have the thing you want.

130.

To *insure* truth in seed, you must, if you purchase, take all the precautions recommended as to *sort of seed*. It will be seen presently, that, to save true seed yourself, is by no means an easy matter. And, therefore, you must sometimes purchase. Find a seedsman that does not deceive you, and stick to him. But, observe, that no seedsman *can* always be sure. He cannot raise *all* his seeds himself. He must trust to others. Of course, he may himself, be deceived. Some kinds of seed will keep a good many years; and, therefore, when you find that you have got some *very true* seed of any sort, get some more of it: get as much as will last you for the number of years that such seed will keep; and, to know how many years the seeds of vegetables and herbs will keep, see paragraph 150.

SOUNDNESS OF SEED.
131.

Seed may be of the right *sort;* it may be *true* to its sort; and, yet, if it be *unsound,* it will not grow, and, of course, is a great deal worse than useless, because the sowing of it occasions loss of time, loss of cost of seed, loss of use of land, and loss of labour, to say nothing about the disappointment and mortification. Here, again, if you purchase, you must rely on the seedsman; and, therefore, all the aforementioned precautions are necessary as to this point also. In this case (especially if the sowing be extensive) the injury may be very great; and, there is no *redress.* If a man sell you *one sort of seed for another;* or, if he sell you *untrue seed;* the *law* will give you redress to the full extent of the injury proved; and the *proof* can be produced. But, if the seed does *not come up,* what *proof* have you? You may prove the *sowing;* but, who is to *prove* that the seed was not *chilled,* or *scorched* in the ground? That it was not eaten by insects there? That it was not destroyed in *coming up,* or in *germinating?*

132.

There are, however, means of ascertaining, whether seed be *sound,* or not, before you sow it in the ground. I know of no seed, which, if sound and really good, will not *sink in water.* The unsoundness of seed arises from several causes. *Unripeness, blight, mouldiness,* and *age,* are the most frequent of these causes. The two first, if excessive, prevent the seed from ever having the germinating quality in them. Mouldiness arises from the seed being kept in a *damp place,* or from its *having heated.* When dried again it becomes light. *Age* will cause the germinating quality to evaporate; though, where there is a great proportion of *oil* in the seed, this quality will remain in it many years, as will be seen in paragraph 150.

133.

The way to *try* seed is this. Put a small quantity of it in *luke-warm* water, and let the water be four or five inches deep. A mug, or basin, will do, but a large tumbler *glass* is best; for then you can *see* the bottom as well as top. Some seeds, such as those of cabbage, radish, and turnip, will, if good, go to the bottom at once. Cucumber, Melon, Lettuce, Endive, and many others, require a few minutes. Parsnip and Carrot, and all the *winged* seeds, require to be worked by your fingers in a little water, and well *wetted,* before you put them into the glass; and the carrot should be *rubbed,* so as to get off part of the *hairs,* which would otherwise act as the feathers do as to a duck. The seed of Beet and Mangel Wurzel are in a *case,* or *shell.* The rough things that we sow are not the *seeds,* but the cases in which the seeds are contained, each case containing from *one* to *five* seeds. Therefore the trial by water is not, as to these two seeds, *conclusive,* though, if the seed be very good; if there be four or five in a case, shell and all will sink in water, after being in the glass an hour. And, as it is a matter of such great importance, that every seed should grow in a case where the plants stand so far apart; as *gaps* in rows of Beet and Mangel Wurzel are so very injurious, the best way is to reject all seed that will not sink case and all, after being put into warm water and remaining there an hour.

134.

But, seeds of all sorts, are, sometimes, if not always, part sound and part unsound; and, as the former is not to be rejected on account of the latter, the *proportion* of each should be ascertained, if a separation be not made. Count then a hundred seeds, taken promiscuously, and put them into water as before directed. If fifty sink and fifty swim, half your seed is bad and half good; and so, in proportion, as to other numbers of sinkers and swimmers. There *may* be plants, the sound seeds of which will *not sink;* but I *know of none.* If to be found in any instance, they would, I think, be found in those of the Tulip-tree, the Ash, the Birch, and the Parsnip, all of which are furnished with so large a portion of wing. Yet all these, if *sound,* will sink, if put into *warm* water, with the wet worked a little into the wings first.

135.

There is, however, another way of ascertaining this important fact, the soundness, or unsoundness of seed; and that is, by *sowing them*. If you have a *hot-bed;* or, if not, how easy to make one for a hand-glass (see Paragraph 94), put a hundred seeds, taken as before directed, sow them in a flower pot, and plunge the pot in the earth, under the glass, in the hot-bed, or hand-glass. The climate, under the glass, is *warm;* and a very few days will tell you what proportion of your seed is sound. But, there is this to be said; that, with strong heat under, and with such complete protection above, seeds may *come up* that would not come up in the *open ground.* There may be enough of the germinating principle to cause vegetation in a hot-bed, and not enough to cause it in the open air and cold ground. Therefore I incline to the opinion that we should try seeds as our ancestors tried Witches; not by fire, but by water; and that, following up their practice, we should reprobate and destroy all that do not *readily* sink.

SAVING AND PRESERVING SEED.

136.

This is a most important branch of the Gardener's business. There are rules applicable to particular plants. Those will be given in their proper places. It is my business here to speak of such as are applicable to *all* plants.

137.

First, as to the *saving* of seed, the *truest* plants should be selected; that is to say, such as one of the most perfect *shape* and quality. In the Cabbage we seek small stem, well-formed loaf, few spare, or loose, leaves; in the Turnip, large bulb, small neck, slender-stalked leaves, solid flesh, or pulp; in the Radish, high colour (if red or scarlet,) small neck, few and short leaves, and long top, the marks of perfection are well known, and none but perfect plants should be saved for seed. The case is somewhat different as to plants, which are some male and others female, but, these present exceptions to be noticed under the names of such plants.

138.

Of plants, the early coming of which is a circumstance of importance, the very earliest should be chosen for seed; for, they will almost always be found to include the highest degree of perfection in other respects. They should have great pains taken with them; the soil and situation should be good; and they should be carefully cultivated, during the time that they are carrying on their seed to perfection.

139.

But, effectual means must be taken to prevent a *mixing* of the sorts, or, to speak in the language of farmers, a *crossing of the breeds.* There can be no cross between the *sheep and the dog:* but there can be between the *dog and the wolf;* and, we daily see it, between the *greyhound and the hound;* each valuable when *true* to his kind: and a cross between the two, fit for nothing but the *rope;* a word which, on this occasion, I use, in preference to that of *halter,* out of respect for the modern laws and usages of my native country.

140.

There can be no cross between a *cabbage and a carrot:* but there can be, between a *cabbage and a turnip;* between a *cabbage and a cauliflower* nothing is more common; and, as to the different sorts of cabbages, they will produce crosses, presenting twenty, and perhaps a thousand, degrees, from the Early York to the Savoy. Turnips will mix with radishes and ruta-baga; all these with rape; the result will mix with cabbages and cauliflowers; so that, if nothing were done to preserve plants true to their kind, our gardens would soon present us with little besides mere herbage.

141.

As to the *causes,* I pretend not to dive into them. As to the *"affectionate feelings"* from which the effect arises, I leave that to those who have studied the "loves of the plants." But, as to the *effect* itself I can speak positively; for, I have now on the table before me an ear of Indian Corn having in it grains of *three distinct sorts;* WHITE CORN, that is to say, colour of bright *rye-straw;* YELLOW CORN, that is to say, colour of a deep-coloured *orange;* SWEET CORN, that is to say, colour of *drab,* and deep-wrinkled, while the other two are plump, and smooth as polished ivory. The *plant* was from a grain of White Corn; but, there were Yellow, and Sweet, growing in the same field, though neither at less than *three hundred yards* distant from the white. The whole, or, at least, the greater part, of the White Corn that grew in the patch was mixed (some ears more and some less) in the same way; and each of the three sorts were mixed with the other two, in much about the same proportion that the White Corn was.

142.

Here we have the different sorts assembled in the same ear, each grain retaining all its distinctive marks, and all the qualities, too, that distinguish it from the other two. Sometimes, however, the mixture takes place in a different way, and the different colours present themselves in *streaks* in all the grains of the ear, rendering the colour of the grains *variegated* instead of their being *one-coloured.*

143.

It is very well known, that effects like this are never perceived, unless in cases where different sorts of Indian Corn *grow at no great distance from each other.* Probably, too, to produce this intermixture, the plants of the several sorts must be all of the same *age;* must all be equal in point of time of blowing and kerning. But, be this as it may, the *fact* of intermixture is certain: and, we have only to know the fact to be induced to take effectual measures to provide against it.

144.

As to *bees* carrying the matter, and *impregnating* plants with it, the idea appears nonsensical; for, how comes it that *whole fields* of Indian Corn are thus mixed? And, in the Indian Corn, let it be observed, the *ear,* that is to say, the *grain-stalk,* is at about *four feet* from the ground, while the *flower* is, perhaps, *eight or ten feet* from the ground! What, then, is the *bee* (which visits only the flower) to carry the *matter* to the flower, and is the flower then to *hand it down to the ear?* Oh, no! this is much too clumsy and bungling work to be believed in. The effect is, doubtless, produced by *scent,* or *smell;* for, observe, the ear is so constructed, and is, at this season, so guarded, so completely enveloped, that it is *impossible* for any *matter* whatever to get at the grain, or at the chest of the grain, without the employment of *mechanical force.*

145.

Away, then, I think we may send all the nonsense about the *farina* of the *male* flowers being *carried to* the female flowers, on which so much has been said and written, and in consequence of which erroneous notion gardeners, in dear Old England, have spent so much time in *assisting* Cucumbers and Melons in their connubial intercourse. To men of plain sense, this is something so inconceivable, that I am afraid to leave the statement unsupported by *proof,* which, therefore, I shall give in a quotation from an English work on Gardening by the REV. CHARLES MARSHALL, Vicar of Brixworth in Northamptonshire. "Setting the fruit is the practice of most *good* gardeners, as generally insuring the embryos from going off, as they are apt to do at an early season; when not much wind can be suffered to enter the bed, and no bees or insects are about, to *convey the farina from the male flowers to the female.* The male flowers, have been *ignorantly* called false blossoms, and so have been regularly pulled off (as said) to strengthen the plants; but they are essential to *impregnate* the female flowers; i. e. those that shew the young fruit at their base: This *impregnation,* called *setting the fruit,* is artificially done thus: as soon as any female flowers are fully open, gather a newly opened male flower, and stripping the leaf gently off from the middle, take nicely hold of the bottom, and *twirling* the top of the male (reversed) over the *centre* of the *female flower,* the fine *fertilizing dust* from the male part will fall off, and adhere to the female part, and *fecundate it,* causing the fruit to keep its colour, *swell,* and proceed fast towards perfection. This business of setting the fruit may be practised through the months of February, March, and April, but afterwards it will not be necessary; for the admission of so much air as may afterwards be given, will disperse the farina effectually; but if the weather still is bad, or remarkably calm, setting may be continued a little longer. If short of male flowers, *one* of them may serve to *impregnate two females!*"

146.

Lest the American reader should be disposed to lament, that such childish work as this is made to occupy the time of English Gardeners, it may not be amiss to inform him, that those to whom the Reverend Gentleman recommends the practising of these mysteries, have plenty of beef and pudding and beer at their masters' expense, while they are engaged in this work of impregnation; and that their own living by no means depends, even in the smallest degree, upon the effect of the application of this *"fine fertilizing dust."* To say the truth, however, there is nothing of *design* here, on the part of the gardener. He, in good earnest, believes, that this operation is useful to the growth of the fruit of his cucumber plants: and, how is he to believe otherwise, when he sees the fact gravely taken for granted by such men as a Clergyman of the Church of England!

147.

Suffice it, now, that we know, that sorts will mix, when seed-plants of the same *tribe* stand *near* each other; and we may easily suppose, that this may probably take place though the plants stand at a considerable distance apart, since I have, in the case of my Indian Corn, given proof of mixture, when the plants were *three hundred yards* from each other. What must be the consequence, then, of saving seed from cucumbers, melons, pumpkins, squashes, and gourds, all growing in the same garden at the same time? To save the seed of *two sorts* of any tribe, in the same garden, *in the same year,* ought not to be attempted; and this it is, that makes it difficult for any *one man* to raise all sorts of seeds good and *true.*

148.

However, *some* may be saved by every one who has a garden; and, when raised, they ought to be carefully *preserved.* They are best preserved *in the pod,* or on the *stalks.* Seeds of many sorts will be perfectly good to the age of eight or ten years, if kept in the pod or on the stalks, which seeds, if threshed, will be good for little at the end of three years or less. However, to keep seeds, without threshing them out, is seldom convenient, often impracticable, and always exposes them to injury from mice and rats, and from various other enemies, of which, however, the greatest is *carelessness.* Therefore, the best way is, except for things that are very curious, and that lie in a small compass, to thresh out all seeds.

149.

They should stand till *perfectly ripe,* if possible. They should be cut, or pulled, or gathered, when it is dry; and, they should, if possible, be dry as dry can be, before they are threshed out. If, when threshed, any *moisture* remain about them, they should be placed in the sun; or, near a fire in a dry room; and, when quite dry, should be put into bags, and hung up against a very dry wall, or dry boards, where they will by no accident *get damp*. The best place is some room, or place, where there is, occasionally at least, a *fire* kept in winter.

150.

Thus preserved, kept from *open air* and from *damp,* the seeds of *vegetables* will keep sound and good for sowing for the number years stated in the following list; to which the reader will particularly attend. Some of the seeds in this list will keep, sometimes, a year longer, if very well saved and very well preserved, and especially if closely kept from exposure to the open air. But, to *lose a crop* from unsoundness of seed is a sad thing, and, it is indeed, negligence wholly inexcusable to sow seed of the soundness of which we are not *certain*.

	Years.		Years.
Artichoke	3	Cauliflower	4
Asparagus	4	Celery	10
Balm	2	Chervil	6
Basil	2	Cives	3
Bean	1	Corn	3
Bean (Kidney)	1	Corn-Salad	2
Beet	10	Coriander	3
Borage	4	Cress	2
Brocoli	4	Cucumber	10
Burnet	6	Dandelion	10
Cabbage	4	Dock	1
Calabash	7	Endive	4
Cale	4	Fennel	5
Cale (Sea)	3	Garlick	3
Camomile	2	Gourd	10
Capsicum	2	Hop	2
Caraway	4	Horse-Radish	4
Carrot	1	Hyssop	6

	Years.		Years.
Jerusalem Artichoke	3	Rape	4
Lavender	2	Rhubarb	1
Leek	2	Rosemary	3
Lettuce	3	Rue	3
Mangle Wurzel	10	Ruta-Baga	4
Marjoram	4	Salsify	2
Marigold	3	Samphire	3
Melon	10	Savory	2
Mint	4	Scorzenera	2
Mustard	4	Shalot	4
Nasturtium	2	Skirret	4
Onion	2	Sorrel	7
Parsley	6	Spinach	4
Parsnip	1	Squash	10
Pea	1	Tansy	3
Pennyroyal	2	Tarragon	4
Potatoe	3	Thyme	2
Pumpkin	10	Tomatum	2
Purslane	2	Turnip	4
Radish	2	Wormwood	2
Rampion	2		

151.

Notwithstanding this list, I always sow *new* seed in preference to *old*, if, in *all* other respects, I know the new to be equal to the old. And, as to the notion, that seeds can be the *better* for being old, even more than a *year* old, I hold it to be monstrously absurd; and this opinion I give as the result of long experience, most attentive observation, and numerous experiments made for the express purpose of ascertaining the fact.

152.

Yet, it is a received opinion, a thing taken for granted, an axiom in horticulture, that *Melon* seed is the *better* for being *old*. MR. MAR-

SHALL, quoted above, in paragraph 145, says, that it ought to be "*about four years old,* though some prefer it *much older.*" And he afterwards observes, that "if new seed only *can be had,* it should be carried a week or two in the *breeches-pocket,* to dry away some of the more *watery* particles!" What should we do here, where no breeches are worn! If age be a recommendation in rules as well as in Melon seed, this rule has it; for, English authors published it, and French authors *laughed at it,* more than *a century past*!

153.

The reader will observe, that, in England, a melon is a *melon;* that they are not, there, brought into market in wagon loads and boat loads, and tossed down in immense heaps on the stones; but, are carried, by twos, or threes, and with as much care as a new-born baby is carried. In short, they are sold at from a dollar to four dollars apiece. This alters the case. Those who can afford to have melons raised in their gardens, can afford to keep a *conjuror* to raise them; and a conjuror will hardly condescend to follow *common sense* in his practice. This would be lowering the profession in the eyes of the vulgar; and, which would be very dangerous, in the eyes of his employer. However, a great deal of this *stuff* is traditionary; and, as was observed before, how are we to find the conscience to blame a gardener for errors inculcated by gentlemen of erudition!

154.

I cannot dismiss this part of my subject without once more cautioning the reader against the danger of *unripe* seed. In cases where winter overtakes you before your seed be quite ripe, the best way is to pull up the plants and hang them by the heels in a *dry, airy* place, till all green depart from the stalks, and until they be quite dry, and wholly rid of juice. Even in hot weather, when the seed would drop out, if the plants were left standing, pull, or cut, the plants, and lay them on a cloth in the sun, till the seed be all ready to fall out; for, if *forced* from the *pod,* the seed is never so good. Seeds will *grow* if gathered when they are *green* as grass, and afterwards dried in the sun; but they do not produce plants like those coming from *ripe seed*. I tried, some years ago, fifty grains of wheat, gathered green, against fifty, gathered ripe. Not only were the *plants* of the former feeble, when compared with the latter; not only was the produce of the former two-thirds less than that of the latter; but even the quality of the grain was not half so good. Many of the ears had *smut*, which was not the case with those that came from the ripened seed, though the land and the cultivation were, in both cases, the same.

SOWING.

155.

The first thing, relating to *sowing*, is, the preparation of the ground. It may be more or less *fine* according to the sort of seed to be sown. Peas and beans do not, of course, require the earth so fine as small seeds do. But, still, the finer the better for *every thing*; for, it is best if the seed be actually *pressed* by the earth in every part; and many seeds, if not all, are best situated when the earth is *trodden down* upon them.

156.

Of course the ground should be *good*, either in itself, or made good by manure of some sort and, on the subject of manure, see Paragraphs 28 and 29. But, in *all cases*, the ground should be *fresh*; that is to say, it should be *dug* just before the act of sowing, in order that the seeds may have the full benefit of the *fermentation*, that takes place upon every moving of the earth.

157.

Never sow when the ground is *wet*; nor, indeed, if it can be avoided, perform any other act with, or on, the ground of a garden. If you dig ground in wet weather, you make a sort of *mortar* of it: it *binds* when then sun or wind dries it. The fermentation does not take place: and it becomes unfavourable to vegetation, especially if the ground be, in the smallest degree, stiff in its nature. It is even desirable, that wet should not come for some days after ground has been moved; for, if the wet come before the ground be *dry at the top,* the earth will *run together,* and will become bound at top. Sow, therefore, if possible, in dry weather, but in freshly-moved ground.

158.

The *season* for sowing will, of course, find a place under the names of the respective plants; and, I do hope, that it is, when I am addressing myself to Americans, unnecessary for me to say, that sowing according to the *Moon* is wholly absurd and ridiculous, and that it arose solely out of the circumstance, that our forefathers, who could not read, had neither Almanack nor Kalendar, to guide them, and who counted by Moons and Festivals instead of by Months and Days of Month.

159.

However, it is necessary to observe, that some, and even many, things, which are usually sown in the Spring, would be better *sown in the fall;* and, especially when we consider how *little time* there is for doing all things in the Spring. Parsnips, carrots, beets, onions, and many other things, may be safely sown in the fall. The seed will not perish, if covered by the earth. But, then, care must be taken to sow early enough in the fall for the plants to *come up* before the frost set in. The seed of all plants will lie safe in this way all the winter, though the frost penetrate to the distance of three feet beneath them, except the seeds of such plants *as a slight frost will cut down.* The seed of kidney beans, for instance, will *rot,* if the ground be not warm enough to *bring it up.* So will the seed of cucumbers, melons, and Indian Corn, unless buried beyond the reach of the influence of the atmosphere. Even early peas would be best sown in the fall, could you have an insurance against *mice.* We all know, what a bustle there is to get in *early peas.* If they were sown in the fall, they would start up the moment the frost were out of the ground, and would be ten days earlier in bearing, in spite of every effort made by the spring-sowers to make their peas overtake them. Upon a spot, where I saved peas for seed, last year, some that was left, in a lock of haulm, at the harvesting, and that lay upon the dry ground, till the land was ploughed late in November, came up, in the spring, the moment the frost was out of the ground, and they were in bloom full *fifteen days* earlier than those, sown in the same field as early as possible in the spring. Doubtless, they would have borne peas fifteen days sooner; but there were but a very few of them, and those standing straggling about; and I was obliged to plough up the ground where they were growing. In some cases it would be a good way, to cover the sown ground with *litter,* or with leaves of trees, as soon as the frost has fairly set in; but, not before; for, if you do it before, the seed may vegetate, and then may be killed by the frost. One object of this fall-sowing, is, to get the work done ready for spring; for, at that season, you have so many things to do at once! Besides, you cannot sow the instant the frost breaks up; for the ground is wet and clammy, unfit to be dug or touched or trodden upon. So that here are ten days lost. But, the seed, which has lain in the ground all the winter, is ready to start the moment the earth is clear of the winter frost, and it is *up* by the time you can get other seed into the ground in a good state. Fall-sowing of seeds to *come up* in the spring is not practised in England, though they there are always desirous to get their things early. The reason is, the uncertainty of their winter, which passes, sometimes with hardly any frost at all; and which at other times, is severe enough to freeze the Thames over. It is sometimes mild till February and then severe. Sometimes it begins with severity and ends with mildness. So that, nine times out of ten, their seed would *come up* and the plants would be destroyed before spring. Besides, they have *slugs* that come out in mild weather, and eat small plants up in the winter. Other insects and reptiles do the like. From these obstacles the American gardener is free. His winter *sets in;* and the earth is safely closed up against vegetation till the spring. I am speaking of the North of Virginia, to be sure; but the gardener to the South will adapt the observations to his climate, as far as they relate to it.

160.

As to the *act of sowing,* the distances and depths differ with different plants, and these will, of course, be pointed out under the names of those different plants; but, one thing is common to all seeds; and that is, that they should be sown in *rows* or *drills;* for, unless they be sown in this way, all is *uncertainty.* The distribution of the seed is unequal; the covering is of unequal depth; and, when the plants come up in company with the weeds, the difficulty of ridding the ground of the latter, without destroying the former, is very great indeed, and attended with *ten times* the labour. Plants, in their earliest state, generally require to be *thinned;* which cannot be done with regularity, unless they stand in rows; and, as to every future operation, how easy is the labour in the one case and how hard in the other! It is of great advantage to almost all plants to move the ground somewhat deep while they are growing; but, how is this to be done, unless they stand in rows? If they be dispersed promiscuously over the ground, to perform this operation is next to impossible.

161.

The great obstacle to the following of a method so obviously advantageous, is, the *trouble.* To draw lines for peas and beans is not deemed troublesome; but, to do this for radishes, onions, carrots, lettuces, beds of cabbages, and other small seeds, is regarded as *tedious.* When we consider the *saving of trouble afterwards,* this trouble is really nothing, even if the drills were drawn one at a time by a line or rule; but, this need not be the case; for, a very cheap and simple tool does the business with as much quickness as sowing at random.

162.

Suppose there be a bed of *onions* to be sown. I make my drills in this way. I have what I call a *Driller,* which is a *rake* six feet long in the head. This head is made of White Oak, 2 inches by 2½; and has *teeth* in it at *eight inches* asunder, each tooth being about six inches long, and an inch in diameter at the head, and is pointed a little at the end that meets the ground. This gives *nine* teeth, there being four inches over at each end of the head. In this head, there is a handle fixed of about six feet long. When my ground is prepared, raked nice and smooth, and cleaned from stones and clods, I begin at the left hand end of the bed, and draw across it *nine rows at once.* I then proceed, taking care to keep the left hand tooth of the Driller in the right hand drill that has just been made; so that now I make but *eight new drills,* because (for a guide) the left hand tooth goes this time in the drill, which was before made by the right hand tooth. Thus, at every draw, I make *eight drills.* And, in this way, a pretty long bed is formed into nice, straight drills in a very few minutes. The sowing, after this, is done with *truth,* and the depth of the covering must be alike for all the seeds. If it be Parsnips or Carrots, which require a wider distance between the rows; or, Cabbage plants, which, as they are to stand only for a while, do not require distances so wide: in these cases, other Drillers may be made. And, what is the expense? There is scarcely an American farmer, who would not make a set of Drillers, for six-inch, eight-inch, and twelve-inch distances, in a winter's day; and, consisting of a *White Oak* head and handle, and of *Locust* teeth, every body knows, that the tools might descend from father to son to the fourth or fifth generation. I hope, therefore, that no one will, on the score of *tediousness,* object to the drilling of seeds in a garden.

163.

In the case of *large pieces of ground,* a hand Driller is not sufficient. Yet, if the land be *ploughed,* furrows might make the paths, the harrow might smooth the ground, and the hand-driller might be used for onions, or for any thing else. However, what I have done for *Kidney Beans* is this. I have a roller drawn by an ox, or a horse. The roller is about eight inches in diameter, and ten feet long, To that part of the frame of the roller, which projects, or hangs over beyond the roller behind, I attach, by means of two *pieces of wood* and *two pins*, a *bar* ten feet long. Into this bar I put *ten teeth;* and near the middle of the bar two handles. The roller being put in motion *breaks all the clods* that the harrow has left, draws after it the *ten teeth,* and the ten teeth make *ten drills,* as deep, or as shallow, as the man chooses who follows the roller, holding the two handles of the *bar.* The two pieces of wood, which connect the bar with the hinder projecting part of the frame of the roller, *work on the pins,* so as to let the bar up and down, as occasion may require; and, of course, while the roller is turning, at the end, the bar, with the teeth in it, is raised from the ground.

164.

Thus are ten drills made by an ox, in about *five minutes,* which would perhaps require a man more than a day to make with a hoe. In short, an ox, or a horse, and a man and a boy, will do twelve acres in a day with ease. And to draw the drills *with a hoe* would require *forty-eight* men at the least; for, there is the *line* to be at work as well as the hoe. Wheat and even Peas are, in the fields, drilled by machines; but *beans* cannot, and especially *kidney beans.* Drills must be made; and, where they are cultivated on a large scale, how tedious and expensive must be the operation to make the drills by line and hoe! When the drills are made, the beans are laid in at proper distances, then covered with a light harrow (*frame* of *White-Oak* and *tines* of *Locust,*) and after all comes the roller, with the teeth lifted up of course; and all is smooth and neat. The expense of such an apparatus is really nothing. The *barrel* of the roller, and the teeth bar, ought to be of *Locust,* which never perishes, and the shafts and frame of White-Oak, which, even without paint, will last a lifetime.

165.

In order to render the march of the ox straight, my ground was ploughed into *lands*, one of which took the ten rows of kidney-beans; so that the ox had only to be kept straight along upon the middle of the land. And, in order to have the lands *flat*, not *arched* at all, the ground was ploughed twice in this shape, which brought the middle of the lands where the furrows were before. If, however, the ground had been flat-ploughed, without any furrow, there would have been no difficulty. I should have started on a straight side, or on the straightest side, leaving out any crook or angle that there might have been. I should have taken two distant objects, two objects, found, or placed, beyond the end of the work, and should have directed the head of the ox in a line with those two objects. Before I started, I should have measured off the width to find where the ox ought to come to again, and then have fixed two objects to direct his coming back. I should have done this at each end, till the piece had been finished.

166.

But, is there no *other use*, to which this roller could be put? Have I not seen, in the *marking* of a corn-field, a man (nay, the farmer himself) mounted upon a horse, which dragged a *log of wood* after it, in order to indicate the lines upon which the corn was to be planted? And have I not, at other times, seen the farmer making these marks, one at a time, with a *plough*? And have I not seen the beauty of these most beautiful scenes of vegetation marred by the crookedness of the lines thus drawn? Now, take my roller, take all the teeth out but *three*, let these three be at four feet apart. *Begin well* on one side of the field; mount your horse: load the teeth well with a stone tied on each; drop the bar; take *two objects* in your eye; go on, keep the two objects in line, and you draw *three lines at once*, all straight and parallel, even if a mile long. Then, turn, and carefully fix the horse again, so that you leave four feet between the outside line drawn before and the inside tooth. You have already measured at the other end (where you started,) and have placed two objects for your guide. Go on, keeping these objects in a line; and you have *three more lines.* Thus you proceed till the field be finished. Here is a great saving of *time;* but, were it for nothing but the *look,* ought not the *log* to give place to the roller?

167.

If I have strayed here out of the garden into the field, let it be recollected, that I write principally for the use of *farmers.* I now return to garden-sowing.

168.

When the seeds are properly, and at suitable distances, placed in the drills, rake the ground, and, in all cases, *tread it with your feet,* unless it be *very moist.* Then rake it *slightly* again; for all seeds grow best when the earth is pressed closely about them. When the plants come up, thin them, keep them clear of weeds, and attend to the directions given under the names of the several plants.

TRANSPLANTING.
169.

The *weather* for transplanting, whether of table vegetables, or of trees, is the same as that for *sowing.* If you do this work in *wet* weather, or when the ground is wet, the work cannot be well done. It is no matter what the plant is, whether it be a cucumber plant, or an oak-tree. It has been observed, as to seeds, that they like the earth to *touch* them in every part, and to lie *close* about them. It is the same with *roots.* One half of the bad growth that we see in *orchards* arises from negligence in the *planting;* from tumbling the earth carelessly in upon the roots. The earth should be *fine* as possible; for, if it be not, part of the roots will remain *untouched* by the earth. If ground be *wet*, it cannot be *fine*. And, if mixed wet, it will remain in a sort of mortar, and will cling and bind together, and will leave more or less of cracks, when it become dry.

170.

If possible, therefore, transplant when the ground is not wet; but, here again, as in the case of sowing, let it be dug, or deeply moved, and well broken, immediately before you transplant into it. There is a *fermentation* that takes place immediately after moving, and a dew arises, which did not arise before. These greatly exceed, in power of causing the plant *to strike*, any thing to be obtained by rain on the plants at the time of planting, or by planting in wet earth. Cabbages and Ruta Baga (or Swedish Turnip) I have proved, in innumerable instances, will, if planted in freshly-moved earth, under a burning sun, be a great deal finer than those planted in wet ground, or during rain. The causes are explained in the foregoing paragraph; and, there never was a greater, though most popular error, than that of *waiting for a shower* in order to set about the work of transplanting. In all the books, that I have read, without a single exception: in the English Gardening books; in the English Farmer's Dictionary, and many other works on English husbandry; in the Encyclopedia; in short, in *all* the books on husbandry and on gardening that I have ever read, English or French, this transplanting in *showery weather* is recommended.

171.

If you transplant in hot weather, the *leaves* of the plants will be scorched; but the hearts will live; and the heat, assisting the fermentation, will produce new roots in twenty-four hours, and new leaves in a few days. *Then* it is that you see fine vegetation come on. If you plant in *wet*, that wet must be followed by *dry*; the earth, from being moved in wet, contracts the *mortary* nature; hardens first, and then cracks; and the plants will stand in a stunted state, till the ground be moved about them *in dry weather*. If I could have my wish in the planting of a piece of Cabbages, Ruta Baga, Lettuces, or, almost any thing, I would find the ground perfectly dry at top; I would have it dug deeply; plant immediately; and have no rain for three or four days. I would prefer no rain for a month to rain at the time of planting.

172.

This is a matter of primary importance. How many crops are lost by the *waiting for a shower*! And, when the shower comes, the ground is either *not dug*, or, it has been dug for some time, and the benefit of the fermentation is wholly lost.

173.

However, there are some very tender plants; plants so soft and *juicy* as to be absolutely burnt up and totally destroyed, stems and all, in a hot sun, in a few hours. Cucumbers and Melons, for instance, and some plants of flowers. These which lie in a small compass, must be *shaded* at least, if not watered, upon their removal; a more particular notice of which will be taken as we proceed in the Lists of the Plants.

174.

In the *act* of transplanting, the main things are to take care not to *bury the heart* of the plant; and to take care that the earth be well pressed about the *point of the root* of the plant. To press the earth very closely about the *stem* of the plant is of little use, if you leave the *point* of the root loose. I beg that this may be borne in mind; for the growth, and even the life, of the plant, depend on great care as to this particular. See *Cabbage*, Paragraph 201, for a minute description of the *act* of planting.

175.

As to the propagation by cuttings, slips, layers and offsets, it will be spoken of under the names of the several plants usually propagated in any of those ways. *Cuttings* are pieces cut off from branches of trees and plants. *Slips* are branches pulled off and slipped down at a joint. *Layers* are branches left on the plant or tree, and bent down to the ground, and fastened, with earth laid upon the part between the plant and the top of the branch. *Offsets* are parts of the root and plant separated from the main root.

CULTIVATION.

176.

Here, as in the foregoing parts of this Chapter, I propose to speak only of what is of *general* application, in order to save the room that would be necessary to repeat instructions for cultivation under the names of the several plants.

177.

The ground being good, and the sowing, or planting, having been properly performed, the next thing is the *after-management*, which is usually called the *cultivation*.

178.

If the subject be from *seed*, the first thing is to see that the plants stand at a proper distance from each other; because, if left too close, they cannot come to good. Let them also be thinned early; for, even while in seed-leaf, they injure each other. Carrots, parsnips, lettuces, every thing, ought to be thinned in the seed-leaf.

179.

Hoe, or weed, immediately; and, let me observe here, once for all, that weeds never ought to be suffered to get to any size either in field or garden, and especially in the latter. In England, where it rains, or drips, sometimes, for a month together, it is impossible to prevent weeds from growing. But in this fine climate, under this blessed sun, who never absents himself for more than about forty-eight hours at a time, and who will scorch a dock-root, or a dandelion-root, to *death* in a day, and lengthen a water-melon shoot 24 inches in as many hours: in this climate, scandalous indeed it is to see the garden or the field infested with weeds.

180.

But, besides the act of killing weeds, *cultivation* means *moving the earth* between the plants while growing. This assists them in their growth: it feeds them: it raises food for their roots to live upon. A mere *flat*-hoeing does nothing but keep down the weeds. The hoeing when the plants are become stout, should be deep; and, in general, with a hoe that has *spanes* instead of a mere flat plate. In short, a sort of *prong* in the *posture* of a *hoe*. And the spanes of this prong-hoe may be longer, or shorter, according to the nature of the crop to be hoed. *Deep-hoeing* is enough in some cases; but, in others, *digging* is necessary to produce a fine and full crop. If any body will have a piece of Cabbages, and will dig between the rows of one half of them, twice during their growth, and let the other half of the piece have nothing but a flat-hoeing, that person will find that the half which has been digged between, will, when the crop is ripe, weigh nearly, if not quite, twice as much as the other half. But, why need this be said in an Indian Corn country, where it is so well known, that, without being *ploughed* between, the corn will produce next to nothing!

181.

It may appear, that, to dig thus amongst growing plants is to cut off, or tear off, their roots, of which the ground is full. This is really the case, and this does great good; for the roots, thus cut asunder, shoot again from the plant side, find new food, and send, instantly, fresh vigour to the plant. The effect of this tillage is quite surprizing. We are hardly aware of its power in producing vegetation; and we are still less aware of the distance, to which the roots of plants extend in every direction.

182.

MR. TULL, the father of the drill-husbandry, gives the following account of the manner, in which he discovered the distance to which certain roots extend. I should observe here, that he was led to think of the drilling of crops in the fields of England, from having, when in France, observed the effects of inner-tillage on the vines, in the vineyards. If he had visited America instead of France, he would have seen the effects of that tillage, in a still more striking light, on plants, in your Indian Corn fields; for, he would have seen these plants spindling, yellow, actually perishing, to-day, for want of *ploughing;* and, in four days after a good, deep, clean and careful ploughing, especially in *hot* weather, he would have seen them wholly change their colour, become of a bright and beautiful green, bending their leaves over the intervals, and growing at the rate of four inches in the twenty-four hours.

183.

The passage, to which I have alluded, is of so interesting a nature, and relates to a matter of so much importance, that I shall insert it entire, and also the *plates,* made use of by MR. TULL to illustrate his meaning. I shall not, as so many others have, take the thoughts, and send them forth as my own; nor, like Mr. JOHN CHRISTIAN CURWEN, steal them from TULL, and give them, with all the honour belonging to them, to *a Bishop.*

184.

"*A Method how to find the distance to which roots extend horizontally.* A piece, or plot, dug and made fine, in *whole hard ground* [*Plate* II. *Fig.* 1.] the end A. 2 feet, the end B. 12 feet, the length of the piece 20 yards; the figures in the middle of it are 20 Turnips, sown early and well hoed. The manner of this hoeing must be, at first, near the plants, with a spade, and each time afterwards, a foot distance, till the earth be once well dug; and, if weeds appear where it has been so dug, hoe them out shallow with the hand-hoe. But, dig all the piece next the out-lines deep every time, that it may be the finer for the roots to enter, when they are permitted to come thither. If the Turnips be all bigger, as they stand nearer to the end B, it is a proof they all extend to the outside of the piece, and the *Turnip* 20, will appear to draw nourishment from six foot distance from its centre. But if the *Turnips* 16, 17, 18, 19, 20, acquire no greater bulk than the *Turnip* 15, it will be clear, that their *roots* extend no farther than those of the *Turnip* 15 does; which is but about 4 foot. By this method the distance of the extent of *roots* of any plant, may be discovered.—There is also another way to find the length of *roots*, by making a long narrow trench, at the distance you expect they will extend to, and fill it with salt; if the plant be killed by the salt, it is certain that some of the roots enter it.

185.

"What put me upon trying this method was an observation of two lands, or ridges (See *Plate* II. *Fig.* 2.) drilled with *Turnips* in rows, a foot asunder, and very even in them; the ground, at both ends and one side, was hard and unploughed. The *Turnips* not being hoed were very poor, small, and yellow, except the three outside rows *b c d* which stood next to the land (or Ridge) *E,* which land, being ploughed and harrowed, at the time the land A ought to have been hoed, gave a dark flourishing colour to these three rows; and the Turnips in the row *d,* which stood farthest off from the new ploughed land *E,* received so much benefit from it, as to grow twice as big as any of the more distant rows. The row *c* being a foot nearer to the new ploughed land, became twice as large as those in *d,* but the row *b,* which was next to the land *E,* grew much larger yet. *E* is a piece of hard whole ground, of about two perch in length, and

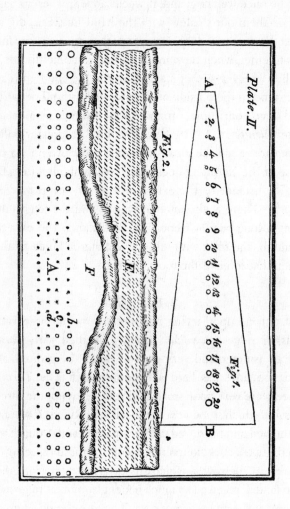

Plate. II.

Fig. 1.

Fig. 2.

about two or three foot broad, lying betwixt those two lands, which had not been ploughed that year; it was remarkable, that during the length of this interjacent hard ground, the rows *b c d* were as small and yellow as any in the land. The *Turnips* in the row *d,* about three foot distant from the land *E,* receiving a double increase, proves they had as much nourishment from the land *E* as from the land A, wherein they stood, which nourishment was brought by less than half the number of *roots* of each of these *Turnips.* In their own land they must have extended a yard all round, else they could not have reached the land *E,* wherein it is probable these few roots went more than another yard, to give each Turnip as much increase as all the roots had done in their own land. Except that it will hereafter appear, that the new nourishment taken at the extremities of the roots in the land *E,* might enable the plants to send out more new roots in their own land, and receive something more from thence. The row *c* being twice as big as the row *d,* must be supposed to extend twice as far; and the row *b,* four times as far, in proportion as it was of a bulk quadruple to the row *d.*"

186.

Thus, then, it is clear, that tillage amongst growing plants is a great thing. Not only is it of great benefit to the plants; not only does it greatly augment the amount of the Crop, and make it of the best quality; but, it prepares the ground for another crop. If a *summer fallow* be good for the land, here is a summer fallow; if the ploughing between Indian Corn *prepares the land for wheat,* the digging between cabbages and other crops will, of course prepare the land for succeeding crops.

187.

Watering plants, though so strongly recommended in English Gardening Books, and so much in practice, is a thing of very doubtful utility in any case, and, in most cases, of positive injury. A country often endures present suffering from long drought; but, even if all the gardens and all the fields could, in such a case, be watered with a watering pot, I much question, whether it would be beneficial even to the crops of the dry season itself. It is not, observe, *rain* water that you can, one time out of a thousand, water with. And, to *nourish plants,* the water must be prepared in clouds and mists and dews. Observe this. Besides, when rain comes, the earth is *prepared* for it by that state of the air, which precedes rain, and which makes all things *damp,* and *slackens* and loosens the earth, and disposes the roots and leaves for the reception of the rain. To pour water, therefore, upon plants, or upon the ground where they are growing, or where seeds are sown, is never of much use, and is generally mischievous for, the air is dry; the sun comes immediately and bakes the ground, and vegetation is checked, rather than advanced, by the operation. The best protector against frequent drought is frequent *digging,* or, in the fields, *ploughing,* and always *deep.* Hence will arise a *fermentation* and *dews.* The ground will have *moisture* in it, in spite of all drought, which the hard, unmoved ground will not. But always dig or plough in *dry weather,* and, the drier the weather, the deeper you ought to go, and the finer you ought to break the earth. When plants are *covered* by *lights,* or are in a *house,* or are covered with cloths in the night time, they may need *watering,* and, in such cases, must have it given them by hand.

188.

I shall conclude this Chapter with observing on what I deem a vulgar error, and an error, too, which sometimes produces inconvenience. It is believed, and stated, that the ground *grows tired,* in time, of the *same sort of plant;* and that, if it be, year after year, cropped with the same sort of plant, the produce will be small, and the quality inferior to what it was at first. Mr. TULL has most satisfactorily *proved,* both by fact and argument, that this is not true. And I will add this fact, that Mr. MISSING, a Barrister, living in the Parish of Titchfield, in Hampshire, in England, and who was a most excellent and kind neighbour of mine, has a border under a south wall on which he and his father before him, have grown *early peas,* every year, for *more than forty years;* and, if, at any time, they had been finer than they were every one year of the four or five years that I saw them, they must have been something very extraordinary; for, in those years (the last four or five of the more than forty) they were as fine, and as full bearing, as any that I ever saw in England.

189.

Before I entirely quitted the subject of *Cultivation,* there would be a few remarks to be made upon the means of preventing the depredations of *vermin,* some of which make their attacks on the *seed,* others on the *roots,* others on the *stem,* others on the *leaves and blossoms,* and others on the *fruit;* but, as I shall have to be very particular on this subject in speaking of *fruits,* I defer it till I come to the Chapter on Fruits.

190.

Having now treated of the Situation, Soil, Fencing, and Laying-out of Gardens; on the making and managing of Hot-Beds and Green-Houses; and having given some directions as to Propagation and Cultivation in general; I next proceed to give Alphabetical Lists of the several sorts of plants, and to speak of the proper treatment for each, under the three heads, *Vegetables and Herbs; Fruits;* and *Flowers.*

IV

Vegetables and Herbs.

191.

The word, VEGETABLES, is not, as was observed in Paragraph 5, quite properly used here. This Chapter treats of the things cultivated in the garden to be eaten at our tables as food; and, they are *Vegetables;* but, a *tree* is also a vegetable; and such is an *herb,* or a *flower.* Therefore, as a distinctive appellation, the word, *vegetables,* is not strictly proper. But, it is the word *we use* to distinguish this class of the products of the earth from others; and, therefore, I use it upon this occasion. HERBS are usually placed as a class separate from *Vegetables;* but, while some of them are merely medicinal, like *Penny-royal,* others are used, not only in medicine and in soups, but also eaten in salads. Therefore, it appeared to be best to bring into this one alphabetical lists, all plants usually grown in a garden, except such as come under the heads of *Fruits,* and *Flowers.*

192.

ARTICHOKE.

A plant little cultivated in America, but very well worthy of cultivation. In its look it very much resembles a *thistle* of the big-blossomed kind. It sends up a seed stalk, and it blows, exactly like the thistle that we see in the *Arms of Scotland*. It is, indeed, a thistle upon a gigantic scale. The parts that are eaten are, the lower end of the thick leaves that envelope the seed, and the bottom out of which those leaves immediately grow. The whole of the head, before the bloom begins to appear, is boiled, the pod leaves are pulled off by the eater, one or two at a time, and dipped in butter, with a little pepper and salt, the mealy part is stripped off by the teeth, and the rest of the leaf put aside, as we do the stem of asparagus. The *bottom,* when all the leaves are thus disposed of, is eaten with knife and fork. The French, who make salads of almost every garden vegetable, and of not a few of the plants of the field, eat the artichoke in salad. They gather the heads, when not much bigger round than a dollar, and eat the lower ends of the leaves above mentioned raw, dipping them first in oil, vinegar, salt and pepper; and, in this way, they are very good. Artichokes are *propagated* from *seed,* or from *offsets.* If by the former, sow the seed in rows a foot apart, as soon as the frost is out of the ground. Thin the plants to a foot apart in the row; and, in the fall of the year, put out the plants in clumps of four, in rows, three feet apart, and the rows six feet asunder. They will produce their fruit the next year. When winter approaches, earth the roots well up; and, before the frost *sets in,* cover all well over with litter from the yard or stable. Open at the breaking up of the frost; dig all the ground well between the rows; level the earth down from the plants. You will find many young ones, or offsets, growing out from the sides. Pull these off, and, if you want a new plantation, put them out, as you did the original plants. They will bear, though later than the old ones, that same year.—As to *sorts* of this plant, there are two, but they contain no difference of any consequence: one has its head, or fruit pod, *round,* and the other, rather *conical.* As to the *quantity* for a family, one row across one of the plats will be sufficient.—For *Jerusalem Artichoke,* see *Jerusalem.*

193.

ASPARAGUS.

Were I writing to Nova Scotians, I ought not to omit to give instructions as to *which end* of the Asparagus the eater ought to use; for, I know a gentleman of that country, who, being at New York, on his first trip from home, began eating at the stem in place of the point. Writing, as I now do, to those, whose country produces, with the least degree of trouble, the finest Asparagus that I ever saw, and probably the finest in the world, no description of the plant, or of its uses, is necessary. But, some remarks on its propagation and cultivation are not wholly unnecessary; for, though it demands less trouble in America than elsewhere, it demands some; and, in proportion as it is valuable and esteemed, it is desirable that the means of procuring it should be well and generally understood.—It is *propagated* from seed. Gather the seed, when it is *dead ripe.* Sow it thinly in drills a foot asunder, and two inches deep, three weeks, or about, before the frost sets in. Press the earth well down upon the seed and, as soon as the frost sets in, but not before, cover the ground with muck, or litter, a foot deep, and lay some boards, or poles, to prevent its blowing off. As soon as the frost breaks up in the spring, take off the litter; and you will have the plants quickly up. (See Paragraph 159.) When the plants are fairly up, thin them to four inches asunder; for, they will be four times as strong at this distance as if they stood close. Keep them clean, and hoe deeply between them all the summer.—To have *beds* of Asparagus, there are two ways of going to work: first, sowing the seed in the beds, at once; and, second, making the beds, and removing the plants into them. It is desirable to have the beds about four feet wide, that you may cut the asparagus by going in the paths between them, and not trample the beds. As to the *first* method, if the soil have a *dry bottom,* trench in the manner described in Paragraph 20; but, in this case, where there is a root always penetrating downward, do not content yourself with a clean trench two feet deep; but, *before you turn your top earth into this trench,* put some good manure into it, and *dig it into this bottom part;* and then you will have manure at *two feet and nine inches from the surface.* Your ground being ready, lay out your beds, four feet wide, with a path two feet wide between each two beds. In the *fall,* having made all the ground right strong with manure, draw the earth to six inches deep *from the top of the beds into the paths,* which will then form high ridges. Then draw your drills *a foot apart,* and sow your seed, as before directed. When they are up, in spring, thin them to *a foot apart.* Thus you will have them a foot apart all over the bed. Keep the plants clean all summer; and, when the haulm is *yellow* in the fall, cut them off near, or close, to the ground; but, let the haulm be *quite dead first;* yet, do it before the frost actually *sets in.* When you have cut off the haulm, lay some litter upon the bed till spring, to prevent the frost from being too long coming out of the ground in spring. When the frost breaks up, throw some wood ashes, or, some other manure about an inch deep over the bed, having first loosened the top of the bed with a fork. Upon this manure, throw earth over the bed, out of the paths, three inches thick, and break it very fine at the time. In the fall, cut down the haulm again as before; repeat the winter operation of littering; and, in the spring again fork up, put on ashes or good mould, and the *other three inches deep of earth* out of the paths. Thus you bring the beds to be an inch or two higher than the paths; and *this year,* if your work have all been well done, you may have some asparagus to eat. The next fall, and every succeeding fall, cut down the haulm and cover with litter as before; and, in the spring, of this third year, put on ashes again, of other fine manure, and throw over the beds the earth that will come out of the paths dug six inches deep. This will make the paths six inches lower than the beds, and that is a great convenience for *weeding,* and for *cutting* the Asparagus. After this, you are to cut down the haulm in the fall, cover with litter during winter, fork up and occasionally manure in the spring, to keep the ground constantly free from weeds, to dig the paths up every fall, and keep them clear from weeds in summer.—The *second method* of making the beds is, to begin with *plants,* instead of seed. The plants (raised as above stated) may be planted in the beds at one year old, or older, if it so happen. Plant them at the same depth that is pointed out for depositing the seed. And, in all other respects, proceed as in the case of a bed begun with seed. As to the time of *beginning to cut,* some say the *third* year, some the *fourth,* and some even the *fifth.* There can be no *fixed time;* for, so much depends on the soil and treatment. Asparagus, like other things, ought to be used when it comes in perfection, and not before.—All that has here been said proceeds upon the supposition that the soil has a *dry bottom.* If a *wet bottom,* sow, or plant, at the *top of the ground,* and, in all other respects proceed as in the case of a dry bottom; except, that the earth to cover the bed with must, time after time, be dug out of the paths, which will, at last, make the paths into ditches, *three feet deep from the tops of the beds.* By these means the roots of the plants will be kept some years longer from reaching the cold, sour soil, at the bottom; for, whenever they *reach that,* the plants, like all others, cease to flourish, and begin to decay.—As to the time that asparagus beds *will last,* that depends on the soil. Having a dry bottom and good management, they will probably last *three generations,* and if that be not enough to compensate the trouble of making them, it would be difficult to find a compensation. The general cause of the decay of Asparagus-beds is, *negligence;* and, particularly, the want of attention to keep them clear of weeds, which, without doubt, are the greatest enemies of the plants. These send their roots down deep; but, they rely also on the ground at the surface. The Lucerne, which will send its roots down *thirty feet* into a dry bottom, and will live in vigour for an age, if kept clean at top; will, though in the best and most suitable soil in the world, perish in a few years, if grass and weeds be suffered to grow amongst it on the surface. Sea-sand, where it can be had, is as good as ashes, *except* the beds are *very near the sea;* and there it is of little use.—With regard to *sorts,* I do not know that there is any difference, except such as *climate produces.* It is very certain, that, to whatever cause owing, the Asparagus here, though so little care is, in general, taken of it, is far superior to that in England. From our frequently meeting with it at a great distance from all houses, there is reason to suppose, that it is a natural weed of the country; and, therefore, it may differ from the English sort, as the *Charlock* and some other weeds do. In England the Charlock has a leaf like that of the *white turnip;* here it has a leaf the colour of that of an early York cabbage; that is to say, of a *blue-green* colour. There may be a difference between the Asparagus of America and that of Europe: at any rate, I will ascertain the fact; for I will carry some seed to England.—As to the space which the beds ought to occupy, that must depend on the size of the family; who are to eat the Asparagus. *Plenty,* however, is always a blessing when the commodity is a good one. About six beds across one of the Plats will be sufficient for any family. They might be at the west end of Plat, No. 6, that being the warmest.—Asparagus may be had in *winter* with the greatest facility. There are but few things that are worth the trouble of a hot-bed for the purpose of having them to eat in their opposite season; but, Asparagus is worth it. And this is the way to have it for the table, even in February, that month of snow and of north-westers. Sow some seed in the garden, in the manner before described, the rows a foot asunder, and the plants four inches apart in the row. Keep them clean, and manure them the first year. Cut the haulm off in the fall. Do not cover them during winter. In the spring fork up the ground, manure it again; and, in the fall cut off the haulm again. Just before the frost sets in, take up as many plants as you will want for your hot-bed. Dig each plant up without tearing it about; and put them all carefully on a cellar floor, cover them over about half a foot thick with fresh ground, and lay some straw upon that to prevent the earth from drying too much. In January prepare dung for a hot-bed; and make the bed in the manner as directed in Paragraphs 69 to 74. When the heat has sufficiently risen, put on earth as in Paragraphs 75 and 76. Upon this earth put your plants, straightening out their roots in every direction. Let the crowns of the roots be about 7 inches apart all over the bed, which, being a bed four feet wide and nine feet long, will contain 180 plants. Cover the plants over with fine earth, so that the surface of this earth be six inches above the crowns of the plants. Proceed as to air, shelter, and covering, in the same way as directed for the cabbage-plants. In about twelve, or fourteen days, you may begin to cut asparagus for the table; and, if you take proper care, and keep your heat up by *a lining* (see Paragraph 93,) you may have a regular supply for a month. When the plants have done bearing here, they are of no use, and may be thrown away. Of all the things that are *forced* in hot-beds, none give so little trouble as Asparagus, and none is so well worth a great deal of trouble.

194.

BALM.

Balm is an herb purely medicinal. A very little of it is sufficient in a garden. It is propagated from seed, or from offsets. When once planted, the only care required is to see that it does not extend itself too far.

195.

BASIL.

Basil is a very sweet annual pot-herb. There are two sorts, the dwarf and the tall. It should be sown in very fine earth, and, if convenient, under a hand-glass. The bunches may be *dried* for winter use.

196.

BEAN.

The only species of bean much used in this country, is that which, in England, is called *Kidney-Bean,* and, in France, *Haricot.* Of these I shall speak in the next article. The Bean I here mean is, what is called by most persons in America the *horse-bean*. In England there are some sorts of this bean used for horses and hogs; but there are several sorts used as human food. It is, at best, a coarse and not very wholesome vegetable; yet some people like it. It is very much eaten by the country people, in England, with their bacon, along with which it is boiled. There are several sorts of these garden-beans, the best of which is the large flat-seeded bean, called the *Windsor-Bean.* The *Long-Pod* is the next best; and, though there are several others, these are enough to mention here.—The bean is difficult to raise here. It does not like *dry and hot weather;* and it likes *moist and stiff land.* If attempted to be raised in America, it should be sown *in the fall* by all means (see Paragraph 159;) but, still it is useless to sow, unless you guard against *mice.* If sown in the South Border, where it would be shaded and protected from the hot sun, it might do pretty well; and the vegetable is convenient as it follows immediately after the early peas are gone.—Ten rows of these beans across the South Border, four feet apart, and the beans four inches apart, will be enough for a family.

197.

BEAN (KIDNEY.)

Endless is the variety of sorts. Some are *dwarfs,* some *climbers;* but, the mode of propagating and cultivating is nearly the same in all, except that the dwarfs require smaller distances than the climbers, and that the latter are grown with poles, which the former are not. In this fine country the seed is so good, the soil and climate so favourable to the plant, the use of the vegetable so general, the propagation and cultivation so easy, and so well understood, that little in detail need be said about them. I prefer sowing the dwarfs in *rows* to sowing them in *bunches* or clumps. It is a great object to have them *early,* and, they may be had much earlier than they usually are with a little pains. It is useless to sow them while the ground is *cold;* for they will not grow till it be warm; but, there are means to be used to get them forwarder than the natural ground will produce them. If you have a *glazed frame,* or a *hand-glass* or two, (see Paragraph 94,) use one or the other in this case; but, if not, dig a hole and put in it, well-shaken together, a couple of wheel-barrows full of good hot dung; and lay some good rich mould upon it six inches thick. Then lay on this some of the earliest sort of dwarf-beans. Put them not more than an inch apart, and cover them with two inches of fine rich mould. Bend some rods over the whole, and put the ends of the rods in the ground; and, every evening, cover this sort of roof over with a bit of old carpet or sail-cloth. In default of these, corn-stalks may do. Do this when the winter frost is just got out of the ground, or soon after. The beans will be up in a week's time; and, in about a fortnight afterwards, they will be fit to remove. The place for them is under a wall, a paling, or a hedge, facing the South. Prepare the ground well and make it rich. Take a spade and carry away a part of the beans at a time, and plant them at six inches asunder with as much earth about the roots as you can. Plant them a little deeper than they stood in the bed. They are very *juicy,* and may have a *little* water given them as soon as planted. Shade them the first day, if the weather be warm and the sun out; and *cover them every night till all frosts be over.* This is easily done, if against any sort of fence, by putting boards, one edge upon the ground and the other leaning against the fence; but, if you have no fence, and have to plant in the open ground, it will be best to plant in clumps, and flower-pots put over the clumps will do for a cover-ing. In Long Island a clod or two, or a brick or two, laid by the side of the clumps, will hold up a large *horse-foot fish shell,* which is an excellent covering. On the *first of June,* 1817, I saw a farmer at South Hempstead, covering his beans with *burr-dock* leaves, while there were hundreds of horse-foot shells in his yard. The dock-leaf would wither in the day. A fresh supply must be had for the next night. This circumstance shows, however, how desirous people are to get this vegetable *early;* and, by the method that I have pointed out, it may be had fifteen days, at least, earlier than it generally is.— As to the *main crop,* it is by no means advisable to sow very early. If you do, the seed *lies long in the ground,* which is always injurious to this plant. The plants come up feebly. The cold weather, that occasionally comes, makes them look *yellow;* and they, then, never produce a fine crop.—Of the various sorts of pole-beans one sowing is enough; for, if you gather as the beans become fit for use, they continue bearing all through the summer, especially the *Lima-*bean, which delights in heat, and for which no weather can be *too dry;* and which should never be sown till the ground be *right warm.* The *Dwarf* sorts may be sown all summer, from the time that the ground becomes warm to within *seven weeks* of the time that the little frosts *begin* in the fall; for, they will, at this season, produce, for eating green, in six weeks from the day of sowing. I sowed them on the 15th of August, and had several gatherings to eat green before the 2d of October when the *first frost* came. They were not *cut up* by the frost till the 17th of October; and they kept bearing till they were.—A row or two sown every fortnight, across one of the *Plats* (see Paragraph 60) will keep any family, however large, well supplied. And, perhaps twenty rows, across one of the Plats, for pole-beans of all the sorts that are desired, will be more than sufficient. It is best to sow several sorts of these; for some bear early and some later than others.—As to the *sorts* of Kidney-beans, they are, as I observed before, almost endless in number. I will, however, name a few: the *Dun,* or *Drab-*coloured dwarf bean, is the earliest. The same ground will bear and *ripen two crops in one year,* the last from the seed of the first. The *Yellow;* the *Black;* the *Speckled;* the *Painted,* white and red: these are all dwarfs; but there are a great many others. Amongst runners, or pole-beans, there are the *Scarlet-blossom,* the seed of which is red and black and the seed-pod rough. There is a *White* bean precisely like the former, except that the bean and blossom are white. The *Case-knife* bean, which, in

England, is called the Dutch-runner: this is the best bean of all to eat green. Then there is the *Cranberry*-bean of various colours as to seed. The *Lima*-bean, which is never eaten green (that is, the *pod* is never eaten,) and which is sometimes called the *butter*-bean, has a broad, flat and thin seed of a yellowish-white colour. This bean must never be sown till the ground is right warm. The other sorts will grow and bear well in England; but this sort will not. I raised good and ripe Indian Corn at Botley; but, I never could bring a Lima-bean to perfection, though I put it in the hottest spot I could find, and though cucumbers produced very well in the natural ground at a yard or two from it.—For the raising of dwarf beans on a large scale, see Paragraphs 163 and 164. The pole-beans *may* be raised in the same way, only with larger spaces (six feet perhaps) between the rows, and *without any poles at all*. The seed *for sale* is raised in this way even in England, where the climate is so cold and wet compared to this. The poling is a great plague and expense; and, if large quantities be raised, it may be dispensed with: nay, it may be dispensed with in a garden; for poles look ugly there; they intercept the view; and the addition they make to the crop is not a compensation even for ill look, especially under this bright sun, where the ground is almost constantly dry.—Let it be observed, that every sort of Kidney-bean must have rich ground to produce a large crop.

198.

BEET.

This vegetable, which is little used in England, is here in as common use as carrots are there. It should be sown in the fall (see Paragraph 159;) but, if not, as soon as the ground is free from frost, and is dry, in the spring. The rows a foot apart, and the plants eight inches apart in the rows. In order to hasten the seed up in the spring (if sown then) soak it four days and nights in rain water before you sow it. Put it two inches deep, cover it well, and press the earth hard down upon it. Sow the seed pretty thick all along the drill; and, when the plants come up, thin them to eight inches apart. Hoe between the plants frequently: but, *not very deep;* because these *tap-rooted* things are apt to *fork* if the ground be made loose very low down while they are growing.—There are yellow and white Beets, as well as *red;* but the red is the *true* kind: the others are degenerate. There is, however, *round* or *turnip-rooted,* red beet, which is equally good with the tap-rooted red-beet.—The ground should be rich, but not fresh dunged. Ashes of wood, or compost mould, is best; and the digging ought to be very deep and all the clods ought to be broken into fine earth; because the clods turn the point of the root aside, and make the tap short, or forked. *Fresh dung,* which, of course, lies in unequal quantities in the ground, invites the tap root, or some of the side roots to it, and thus causes a short or forked beet, which, for several reasons, is not so good as a long and smooth one.—As to the preserving of beets during the winter, it is well known, that the way is to put them in a dry cellar, with dry sand between them, or indeed, without sand or any thing at all between them. They may, if in large quantities, and not wanted till spring, be preserved out of doors, thus: Take them up three weeks before the hard frost is to come. Cut off their leaves; let them lay two or three days upon straw, or boards, to dry in the sun; then lay a little straw upon the ground, and, in a fine dry day, place *ten bushels* of beets (picking out all the *cut* or *bruised* ones) upon it in a conical form. Put a little straw smoothly over the heap; then cover the whole with six or eight inches of earth; and place a green turf at the top to prevent the earth from being washed, by rain, from the point, before the frost set in. All the whole heap will *freeze* during the winter; but, the frost will not injure the beets, nor will it injure *Carrots,* preserved in the same way.—If you have more than ten bushels, make another heap, or other heaps; for fear of *heating* before the frost comes. When that comes, all is safe till spring; and, it is in *the spring,* that season of *scarcity,* for which we ought to provide. How many bushels of beets are flung about and wasted in the fall, the smallest of which would be a treat in the month of May!—As to the *quantity* to be raised for a family, eighteen rows, planted as above, across one of the Plats (little more than two perches of ground) will produce 812 beets, or nearly *four for each day*, from the first of November to the last of May; and, if they are of the size that they ought to be, here are much more than enough. Beets may be *transplanted*, and will, in that way, get to a good size. See Transplanting, Paragraph 169.

199.

BROCOLI.

This plant is not much cultivated in America; and, indeed, scarcely at all. In England it is grown in great quantities, especially near London. It is there sown in the spring, and eaten in the fall and during the winter, even until spring. It is of the nature of the *Cauliflower*, which see. One sort has a whitish head, and is like a cauliflower, except that the white is a *yellow-white*. Another sort has a *purple* head; and there is another of a *greenish* hue. It is cultivated, in all respects like a Cabbage (which see;) but, as it is *large*, it must be placed at wider distances, not less than two feet and a half each way. If raised *very early* in the spring and planted out in June, and in good ground, as *cool* as can be got, it will have heads in *October*; and, if any of the plants have not then perfected their heads, when the *hard* frost is coming, they may be treated like those of the spring-sown cauliflowers which have not perfected their heads at this season.— *Fifty* of this plant, for the fall, may be enough; and they ought to be planted out in the *South Border* in order to be kept as cool as possible. The *white* sort is deemed the *handsomest;* but, the others are *more hardy*.—To have Brocoli *in the spring;* that is to say, in *May* (for New York) is *the thing!* The thing *may* be done; for I had some pretty good in May 1818.—Sow in *June*. Transplant in July; put the plants at 2½ feet apart. Till well between; and earth up the stems of the plants in August. They will be very tall and stout, in good ground, in November; and a sharp frost or two will not hurt them. But, to keep them *through the winter* is a troublesome thing. Nevertheless, to have them at New York or Boston *in May,* and, at Philadelphia late *in April;* to have something little short of a cauliflower at that season, is worth some trouble, and even some expense; for, at that very season, the people of New York, are carrying home *wild dock leaves* from *market,* bought at three or four cents a handful! This is the way to go to work to have Brocoli at this season. *Five rows,* across one of the *Plats* in the garden, will contain 110 plants. The space they will occupy will be 56 feet long, and 10½ feet wide from out-side row to out-side row. Now, *all this space* must have *a covering* during the time that the ground is completely *locked up* by the frost. And this is the way to cover it. Before the ground be hard frozen, put some *stout* stakes in the ground on both out-sides of the out-side rows, and at about a foot from the stems of the plants. Let these stakes be about a foot higher than the *tops of the leaves* of the plants; and that will make the stakes about four feet high. Let these stakes (which should not be less than three inches through) have a *fork* at the upper end to lodge a pole upon to go from stake to stake *across the plantation.* That these poles may not bend in the middle, by-and-by, when the covering is put on, put another row of forked stakes along the middle, or near the middle of the plantation. From out-side row of stakes to out-side row of stakes will be twelve feet and a half. The stakes are to be four feet asunder in the long rows, and they will be about six feet asunder across the plantation. Lay *stout* poles across, and let each pole rest in the forks of the three stakes. Then tie some stout *rods* longways upon the poles, at about nine inches from each other. Then some small rods across them at nine inches from each other. Then tie small rods along the sides and at the ends from stake to stake, nine inches apart, and upright rods against these, nine inches apart. Thus you have a sort of net-work over the whole plantation. And, there let it stand, till the rains are over, and until the winter is *fairly set* in, which, at New York, may be about Christmas. When all is frozen *hard up,* cover *close* over the lattice work a foot thick with straw, at the *least,* and lay on something to prevent the straw from moving. Then *set up* straw, or corn stalks, against the sides and the ends of the erection. Place the straw or stalks a foot thick at least, and fasten them well up, so as to keep out, not the frost, but *all light* and all occasional *thaws* from entering. Thus let the whole remain till the *breaking up* of the frost: and then *take all away.* Do not wait till the frost is *out of the ground;* but, take away as soon as the grand *breaking up* comes. You will find the plantation as *green* as it was when you closed it up. This will be about the middle of March (Long Island;) and though there will be many and sharp frosts after this, these will not injure the plants. As soon as the ground is *dry at top,* hoe *deep* amongst the plants; hoe again in about ten days; and again in another ten days; and, about the *first week in May,* or in the second at latest, you will *begin* to cut Brocoli to eat. The heads will come in one after another; and, recollect, that you have 110 heads, which is nearly 4 *a day for a month;* and this, you will observe, at a season, when people are glad to *buy* dock-leaves to eat! When we talk of *trouble,* what is trouble but *labour;* and what is labour but a thing to be *bought?* I am supposing a case where a *gardener* is kept; and, pray, what has he else to do? But, suppose a man to be hired expressly, would he not go to the wood and get the materials and make the lattice work in *a day?* Would it take him more than another day to lay on the straw! Here, then, are *two dollars;* and, supposing the straw and the stakes and poles and rods to be *bought,* the straw would be nearly as good for litter afterwards, and the poles, stakes and rods would last for many years, if tied up in bundles and laid safely away from winter to winter.

200.

BURNET.

Burnet is a well known grass, or cattle plant. It is used by some in salads. When bruised, or cut, it smells like *cucumber.* It is a perennial, and a very poor thing.

201.

CABBAGE.

The way to raise Cabbage-Plants in a *hot-bed* has been given in Paragraphs 77 to 96.—In the open ground you may put your seed rows at six inches distance, and put the seeds *thin* in the row. As soon as up, thin the plants to three inches in the row. The next thing is *transplanting;* and I will speak of that before I speak of seasons, sorts, and preserving during winter.—Of the preparation and state of the ground, and of the proper weather for transplanting, I have spoken in Paragraphs 169 to 175. Read those paragraphs carefully again, and bear their contents in mind. But, to have *fine* cabbages, of any sort, the plants must be *twice* transplanted. First, they should be taken from the seed bed (where they have been sown in drills near to each other,) and put out into fresh-dug, well broken ground, at six inches apart every way. This is called *pricking* out. By standing here about fifteen or twenty days, they get straight and strong, stand erect, and have a straight and stout stem. Out of this plantation they come nearly *all of a size;* the roots of all are in the same state; and, they strike quicker into the ground where they are to stand for a crop.—But, if you do not, whether from negligence or want of time, prick your plants out, choose the strongest, if you do not want them all; and, at any rate, do not plant strong and weak promiscuously, but put each by themselves. If you do not *intend* to prick out, leave the plants *thinner* in the seed bed, and hoe deep between them while they stand there. Besides this you may pass a *sharp* spade along under the rows, and cut off the top-roots; for they must be shortened when the plants are transplanted. This, if done a week or ten days before transplanting will give the plants a more *bushy root;* and will, in some measure, supply the place of pricking out.— Having the plants ready for transplanting; and having the ground and weather as described in Paragraph 170, you proceed to your work, thus: *dig* the plants up, that is, loosen the ground under them with a spade, to prevent their being stripped too much of their roots. Put them in *rows* of course. The *setting-stick* should be the upper part of a spade or shovel handle. The eye of the spade is the handle of the stick. From the bottom of the eye to the point of the stick should be about nine inches in length. The stick should not be *tapering;* but nearly of equal thickness all the way down, to within an inch and a half of the point, where it must be tapered off to the point. If the wood be cut away all round, to the thickness of a dollar, and *iron* put round in its stead, it makes a very complete tool. The iron becomes bright, and the earth does not adhere to it, as it does to wood. Having the plant in one hand, and the stick in the other, make a hole suitable to the root that it is to receive. Put in the root in such way as that the earth, when pressed in, will be on a level with the butt-ends of the lower, or outward, leaves of the plant. Let the plant be rather higher than lower than this; for, care must be taken not to put the plant so low as for the earth to fall, or be washed, into the *heart* of the plant, nor even into the inside of the bottom leaves. The stem of a cabbage, and stems of all the cabbage kind, send out roots from all the parts of them that are put beneath the surface of the ground. It is good, therefore, to plant as deep as you can without injury to the leaves.—The next consideration is, the *fastening of the plant in the ground.* I cannot do better than repeat here what I have said in my Year's Residence, Paragraphs 83 and 84. "The hole is made deeper than the length of the roots; but the root should not be *bent* at the point, if it can be avoided. Then, while one hand holds the plant, with its root in the hole, the other hand applies the setting stick to the earth on one side of the hole, the stick being held in such a way as to form a sharp triangle with the plant. Then, pushing the stick down, so that its point go *a little deeper than the point of the root,* and giving it a little *twist,* it presses the earth against the *point,* or *bottom* of the root." And thus all is safe, and the plant is sure to grow. The general, and almost universal, fault, is, that the planter, when he has put the root into the hole, draws the earth up against the *upper part* of the root, and, if he press pretty well there, he thinks that the planting is well done, But, it is the point of the root against which the earth ought to be pressed, for there the fibres are; and, if they do not *touch the earth closely,* the plant will not thrive. To know, whether you have fastened the plant well in the ground, take the tip of one of the leaves of the plant between your finger and thumb. Give a pull. If the plant resist the pull, so far as for the bit of leaf to come away, the plant is properly fastened in the ground; but, if the pull bring up the plant; then you may be sure that the planting is not well done. The point of the stick ought to twist and press the earth up close to the *point of the root,* so that there be *no hollow* there. Pressing the earth up against the *stem* of the plant is of little use. As to *distances* they must be proportioned to the size which the cabbages usually come to; and the size (difference of soil out of the question) varies with the *sort.* However, for the very small sorts, the *Early Dwarf,* and the Early *Sea-Green,* a foot apart in all directions is enough; for there is no occasion to waste garden ground; and you do not want such things to stand long, and the plants are in plenty as to number. The next size is the *Early York,* which may have 16 inches every way. The *Sugar-loaf* may have 20 inches. The *Battersea* and *Savoy* two feet and a half. The large sorts, as the *Drum-head* and others, 3 feet at least. Now, with regard to *tillage,* keep the ground clear of weeds. But, whether there be weeds or not, hoe between the plants in ten days after they are planted. The reasons for this are amply stated in Paragraphs 176 to 186. You cannot *dig* between the plants, which stand at the smallest distances; but you may, and ought, to dig once, if not twice, during their growth, between all the rest. To prevent a sudden check by breaking all the roots at once, in hot weather, dig *every other interval,* leave the rest, and dig them a week later. All the larger sorts of cabbages should, about the time that their heads are beginning to form, be *earthed* up; that is, have the earth from the surface draw up against the stem; and, the taller the plants are, the more necessary this is, and the higher should the earth be drawn. After the earth has been thus drawn up from the surface, *dig,* or *hoe deep,* the rest of the ground.—Thus the crop will be brought to perfection.—As to *sorts,* the earliest is the *Early Dwarf,* (sometimes called the *Early Salisbury;*) the next is the *Early Sea Green;* then comes the *Early York.* Perhaps any one of them may do; but the first will head ten days sooner than the last. The *Sugar-loaf,* sweetest and richest of all cabbages, if sown and transplanted when Early Yorks are, will head nearly a month later. It is an excellent cabbage to come in in July and August. Some sown three weeks later will carry you through September and October; and some sown in June and transplanted in July, will carry you on till Christmas. For the winter use, there really needs nothing but the *Dwarf Green Savoy.* When good and true to kind it is very *much curled* and of a *very deep green.* It should be sown as soon as the ground is at all warm, and planted out as soon as stout enough. By November it will have large and close heads weighing from 5 to 8 pounds each. This is the best of all winter-cabbages. If you have *Drum-heads,* or other large cabbages, the time of sowing and that of transplanting are the same as those for the Savoy. But, let me observe here, that the early sorts of cabbage keep, during winter, as well as the large, late sorts. It is an error to suppose, that those cabbages only, which will not come to perfection till the approach of winter, will *keep well.* The Early York, sown in June, will be *right hard* in November, and will keep as well as the Drum-head, or any of the *coarse* and *strong-smelling* cabbages. The Early Yorks are not so *big* as the Drum-heads; but, observe, that as the former require but 16 inches distance, and the latter 3 feet, *five* of the former stand on the ground of *one* of the latter. So that, perhaps, the Early Yorks will be the largest *crop* after all. I have tried the *keeping of both;* and I know that the fine Cabbages keep as well as the coarse ones. The *Red Cabbage* is raised and cultivated in the same season and same manner as the *Green Savoy.* There are many other sorts of cabbage, early as well as late; and they may be tried; but those above-mentioned are certainly sorts enough for any family.—The *preserving* of cabbages during the winter is all that remains to be treated of under the word cabbage; but, as every reader must know, it is a matter of great importance; for on it depends the supply of cabbages for *four months* in the year, North of Virginia and South of Boston, and for *six* months in the year when you get as far North as the Province of New Brunswick.—The *cellar* is a poor place. The *barn* is worse. The cabbages get *putrid* parts about them. If green vegetables be not fed from the earth, and be in an unfrozen state, they will either *wither* or *rot*. Nothing is nastier than *putrid* cabbage; and one rotten cabbage will communicate its offensiveness to a whole parcel. Pits you cannot open in winter. To *turn the heads* down and cover them with earth while the root stands up in the air, is liable to the same objection. The cabbages are pretty safe; but you cannot *get at them* during the winter. I have tried all the ways that I ever saw practised, or that I ever heard of; and the following method I found to answer every purpose; it is the surest preservation, and gives the least trouble, whether in the putting together or in the taking away for use.—Lay out a piece of ground, four feet wide, and in length proportioned to your quantity of cabbages to be preserved. Dig, on each side of it, a little trench, a foot deep, and throw the earth up on the four-feet bed. Make the top of the bed level and smooth. Lay some poles, or old rails, at a foot apart, long-ways, upon the bed. Then put some smaller poles, or stout sticks cross ways on the rails or poles, and put these last at five or six inches apart. Upon these lay, corn-stalks, broomcorn stalks, or twigs or brush of trees, *not very thick,* but sufficiently thick just to cover all over. Make the top flat and smooth. Then, just as the frost is about to *lock up* the earth, take up the cabbages, knock all dirt out of their roots, take off all dead or yellow looking leaves, and some of the outside leaves besides; put the cabbages, head downwards, upon the bed, with their roots sticking up; and cover them with straw so thick as for the straw to come up nearly to the root of the cabbage. Do not pack them quite close. It is better if they do not touch each other much. Lay some bits of wood, or brush-wood, to prevent the straw from blowing off. If the frost *catch you,* before you have got the cabbages up, *cut* them off close to the ground, and let the stumps, instead of the roots, stick up through the straw.—Out of this stack you will take your cabbages perfectly *green* and *good* in the spring, when the frost *breaks up;* and to this stack you can, at all times in the winter, go, with the greatest facility, and get your cabbages for use, which you can to no other species of conservatory that I ever saw or heard of. The *hollow* part below the cabbages takes away all wet that may come from occasional rains or meltings of snow; and the little ditches on the sides of the bed keep the bed itself free from being soaked with wet. Even if deep snows come and lie for months, as in Nova-Scotia, New Brunswick, and Canada, it is only removing the snow a little; and here are the cabbages always *fresh* and good.—Immense quantities, particularly in woody countries, may be stacked and preserved in this way, at a very trifling expense. In fields the side trenches would be made with the *plough;* poles, in such a case, are of all sizes, always at hand; and, *small* brush wood might do very well instead of straw, *fir*-boughs, *laurel*-boughs, or *cedar*-boughs, would certainly do better than straw; and where is the spot in America, which has not one of these three?—*Cabbage Stumps* are also to be *preserved;* for they are very useful in the spring. You have been cutting cabbages to eat in October and November. You leave the stumps standing, no matter what be the *sort.* Take them up before the frost sets in; trim off the long roots, and lay the stumps in the ground, in a *sloping* direction, row behind row, with their heads four or five inches out of ground. When the frost has just *set in* in *earnest,* and not before, cover the stumps all over a foot thick or more, with straw, with corn-stalks, or with evergreen boughs of some sort. As soon as the breaking-up comes, take off the covering, and stir the ground (as soon as dry,) by hoeing amongst the stumps. They should be placed in an *early spot;* in one of the warmest places you have; and they will give you (at New York) an abundance of fine greens towards the end of April, when a handful of wild *dock-leaves* sells in New York market for *six-pence* York money, which is rather more than an English three pence.—*Lastly,* as to the saving of *cabbage seed.* The cabbage is a *biennial.* It brings its flower and its seed the *second year.* To have cabbage seed, therefore, you must preserve the cabbage, head, root and all, throughout the winter; and this must be done, either in a *cellar,* or under covering of some sort out of doors; for, the root must be *kept in the ground all winter.* It is possible, and, I think, likely, that seed from the *stump* is just as good as any; but as one single cabbage will give seed enough for any garden for three, four, or five years, the little pains that the preservation can require is not worth the smallest risk.—As to the *quantity* of cabbages wanted for a family, it must depend on the size of the family and on their taste.

202.

CALABASH.

An annual. Cultivated like the *cucumber,* which see.

203.

CALE.

This is of the cabbage kind. There are several sorts of it: and, it is, in all respects propagated and cultivated like the *Green Savoy,* which see under *Cabbage.*—The Cale does not *head,* or *loave,* but sends forth a loose, open top, which in England, is used after the frost has pinched it, and then it sends out side-shoots from its tall stem, which it continues to do, if kept cropped, till May. In mild winter climates it is very useful and pleasant. It does not get rotted by the successive freezings and thawings, as cabbages do. It is always *green* and fresh. Backward-planted savoys, may, perhaps, be as good; but the Cale is very good too. It will, I dare say, stand throughout *some* winters as far North as Philadelphia. It is worth trying; for *greens* are very pleasant in winter.—The *Curled* Cale is the best.—

Its seed is saved like that of the cabbage.—There is a sort of Cale called *Boorcole,* and a whole list of things of somewhat the same kind, but to name them would be of no use.

204.

CALE (SEA.)

This is a capital article. Inferior in point of quality to no vegetable but the *Asparagus,* superior to that in the merit of *earliness;* and, though of the easiest possible propagation and cultivation, I have never seen any of it in America.—It is propagated by *seed,* and also by *offsets.* The seeds may be sown, or the young plants (at a year old) planted, or the *offsets* (or little shoots from the sides of the stems) planted, on the spot where the crop is to be produced.— The mode of cultivation is in *beds, precisely the same in all respects as Asparagus;* except, that the Cale may be begun upon the *second* year. Cover the beds *thick* with litter in winter; so that the frost may not enter very deep; and, in April (Long Island) you will have plenty.—The moment it *peeps* out, cut it, and you have a white stalk seven or eight inches long, which is cooked just as asparagus is, and is all eaten from top to bottom. This plant is a native of the sea beach; and is as hardy as any weed that grows. Instead of *earth,* you may, if convenient, lay sand (and especially *sea sand*) for it to shoot up through. It may be moved at any age of the plant. Any old stump of it will grow. After you leave off cutting it in the spring, it goes shooting on, and, during the summer it bears seed. In the fall the stalks are cut down, and you proceed with the beds as with those of Asparagus.—Two beds across any one of the plats are enough for any family.—This is, unquestionably, (after the Asparagus,) the very best garden vegetable that grows. Sea Cale may be had at any time in winter, as easily as Asparagus (which see,) and with less care. The roots may be dug up in the fall and thrown under any shed with litter, or straw, over them, till you want them. The earth in the hot-bed must be *deeper* than for Asparagus:

that is all the difference.—The seed is saved as easily as that of Asparagus.

205.
CAMOMILE.

Camomile is a medicinal herb of great use. It is a perennial, and, though it may be propagated from seed, it is easiest propagated by parting the roots. One little bit of root will soon make a bed sufficient for a garden. The *flowers* are used in medicine. They should be gathered before they begin to fade: and be dried in a gentle sun, or in shade; and then put by, in paper bags, in a dry place.

206.
CAPSICUM (OR PEPPERS.)

An annual plant, sown early in fine earth, in drills a foot apart, and at six inches apart in the drills. It is handsome as a *flower*, and its pods are used as a pickle.

207.
CARAWAY.

The seeds are used in cakes. The plant is an annual. Sow in the spring, in fine rich ground, and leave the plants eight inches apart each way.

208.
CARROT.

Read the Article BEET; for, the same season, same soil, same manure, same preparation for sowing, same distances, same intercultivation, same time of taking up, and mode of preserving the crop, all belong to the *Carrot*.—About the same quantity also is enough for a large family.—Some fine roots may be carefully preserved to plant out for seed in the spring; and the seed should be taken only from the *centre* seed-stalks of the carrots; for that is the finest.—The mark of a good kind of seed, is, *deep*-red colour of the tap. The paler ones are degenerate; and the *yellow* ones, are fast going back to the wild carrot. Some people consider that there are *two sorts:* I never could discover any difference in the plants coming from seed of what has been called the *two sorts.* A Cow will nearly double her milk, if taken from common pasture in *October,* and fed well on carrot-*greens,* or tops; and they may, at this season, be cut off for that purpose. They will shoot a little again before the time for taking the carrots up; but, that is of no consequence. These shoots can be cut off before the carrots be put away for winter. Carrots will *transplant* like Beets; but, they grow still more *forked* than the Beet in this case. They do, however, grow large and heavy in this way. I have had some weigh more than three pounds.

209.

CAULIFLOWER.

It is not without *some* difficulty, that this plant is brought to perfection in any country, where the frost is severe in winter, and especially where the summers are as hot as they are in every part of the United States. Still it *may* be brought to perfection.—It is a *cabbage,* and the French call it the *flower-cabbage.* Its head is a lump of rich pulp, instead of being, as a cabbage-head is, a parcel of leaves folding in towards a centre, and lapping over each other. The Cauliflower is an *annual* plant. It blows, and ripens its seed, during the year that it is sown; and, in fact, the part which is eaten is not, as in the cabbage, a lump of *leaves,* but the *seed stalks, pods,* and blossoms, in their embryo and compact state, before they expand.—It is the same with *Brocoli.*—Cauliflowers may be had to eat in the fall, or in the spring. The last is the most difficult to accomplish; and I will, therefore, treat first of the means of accomplishing that.—To have Cauliflowers to eat in the spring, that is to say, in *June,* you must sow them in the *fall;* for, they will have a certain *age* before their heads will come. Yet, they are very *tender.* They will not endure a South of England winter without a *covering,* occasionally at least, of some sort; and the covering is, almost always, *glass*, either on frames or in a hand-light. So that, to keep them through an American winter, there must not only be glass, but that *glass* (except where you have a green-house to be kept warm by fire) must have a *covering* in severe weather.—They require *age*, and yet, you must not sow them *too early* in the fall; for, if you do, they will have little heads about the size of a dollar, and go off *to seed* at once without coming to a large head at all. If you be too *backward* in sowing, the heads do not *begin* before the *great heat* comes; and, in that case, they will not head *till the fall*.—All these circumstances make the raising of them for spring use very difficult.—Sow (Long Island) *first week*, or *second week*, in *September*, in the same manner that you sow cabbages. When the plants have *eight leaves*, put them in a warm place, in the *natural ground*, and do not put much dung in the ground. The back part of the Hot-bed ground would be the place. Plant them six inches asunder upon a piece of ground that your *frame will cover*; but do not put on the frame, till *sharpish* frosts begin to come. Then put it on, and, whenever you expect a frost, put over the *lights at night*. If there be much rain, keep the lights on, but give plenty of air. Take the lights off whenever you can. When the *hard* frost comes, put long dung from the stable very thick all round the frame up to the very top of it, and extending a yard wide; and, in *severe weather*, cover the glass with a mat, or old carpet first; then put straw upon the mat; and then cover the straw with another mat. But, mind, they must be kept *in the dark* as little as possible. When the sun is out, they must have it; and, in mild days, they must have a great deal of air. When there is an occasional *thawing day*, take the lights *off*, and hoe and stir the ground; for, they want *strength* as well as protection; and they must have all the air you can, with safety to their lives, give them.— Thus you go on till within about *three weeks of the general Indian-Corn planting season*. By this time you may leave the lights off day and night. Ten days before Corn-planting get your ground ready, deeply dug and full of rich manure. Make holes with a spade; remove each plant with a ball of earth about the roots; fix the plants well in the holes at two feet asunder; leave a little dish round each; water them with water that runs out of a yard where cattle are kept. They love moisture, especially under a hot sun. Give them this sort of water, or muddy, stagnant water, every three days in hot weather; hoe and dig between them also; and, you will have Cauliflowers in June.—If you have a Green-house, the trouble is little. Sow as before. Put about four plants in a flower-pot a foot diameter at top, instead of putting under a frame. They will live in the Green-house like other plants; and will be ready to put out as above-mentioned. Fifty plants are enough. They are very fine vegetables; but they come not earlier than *green peas.*—To have Cauliflowers to eat *in the fall* is a much easier matter, and then they are, in my opinion, *more valuable* than in the spring. Sow at the same time and in the same manner as you sow early cabbages. Treat the plants in the same way; put them at two feet and a half distance; you need not now water them; they will begin to come early in October; and, if any of them have not perfected their heads when the *sharp* frosts come, take them up by the root, hang them up by the heels in a *warm* part of a barn, or in a cellar; they will get tolerably good heads; and you will have some of those heads to eat *at Christmas.*—The seed, on account of the *heat,* is extremely difficult to save in America; but, if a fall Cauliflower were kept in a Green-house during winter, and put out three weeks before corn-planting time, I am persuaded, it would bring good seed in June.—The *quantity* of this plant must depend upon the taste for it; but it is so much better than the very best of cabbages, that it is worth some trouble to get it.

210.

CELERY.

The qualities of this plant are universally known. There are three or four sorts. The *white,* the *red,* the *hollow,* and the *solid.* The *hollow white* is the best; but the propagation and cultivation of all are the same. The whole of that part of the year, during which the frost is out of the ground, is not a bit too long for the getting of *fine* Celery. The seed, sown in the cold ground, in April, will lie *six weeks before it come up.* A wheel-barrow full of hot dung, put in a hole in the ground against a wall, or any fence, facing the south, and covered with rich and fine mould, will bring the seed up in *two weeks.* If you have a hot-bed frame, or a hand-light, the thing is easy. A large flower-pot will bring up out of ground, plants enough for any family. As soon as the plants are *three inches high,* and it scarcely matters how thick they stand, make a nice little bed in open free air; make the ground rich and the earth very *fine.* Here prick out the plants at 4 inches apart; and, of course, 9 in a square foot. They are so very small, that this must be carefully done; and they should be gently watered once, and shaded 2 days. A bed 10 feet long and 4 wide will contain 360 plants: and, if they be well *cultivated,* they are more than any common-sized family can want from November till May.—In this bed the plants stand till the middle of July, or thereabouts, when they are to go out into trenches. Make the trenches a foot deep and a foot wide, and put them not less than *five feet* asunder. The ground that you make the trenches in should not be fresh-dug; but be in a *solid state,* which very conveniently may be; for Celery comes on just as the Peas and early Cabbages and Cauliflowers have gone off. Lay the earth that you take out in the *middle* of the space between the trenches, so that it may not be washed into them by the heavy rains; for it will, in such case, cover the hearts of the plants, and will go very nearly to destroy them.—When you have made your trench, put along it some good rich compost manure, partly consisting of *wood ashes.* Not *dung;* or, at least, not dung fresh from the yard; for, if you use that, the celery will be *rank* and *pipy,* and will not keep nearly so long or so well.—Dig this manure in, and break all the earth very fine as you go.—Then take up your plants, and trim off the long roots. You will find, that every plant has offsets to it, coming up by the side of the main stem. Pull all these off, and leave only the single stem. Cut the leaves off so as to leave the whole plant about six inches long.—Plant them, six inches apart, and fix them in the manner so minutely dwelt on under the article, *Cabbage,* keeping, as you are at work, your feet close to the outside edges of the trench. Do not *water* the plants; and, if you plant in *fresh-dug* ground, and fix your plants well, none of the troublesome and cumbrous business of *shading* is at all necessary; for the plant is naturally hardy, and, if it has heat to wither it above, it has also that heat beneath to cause its roots to strike out almost instantly.—When the plants begin to grow, which they quickly will do, *hoe* on each side and between them with a small hoe. As they grow up, *earth their stems;* that is, put the earth up to them, but not too *much at a time;* and let the earth that you put up be finely *broken,* and not at all *cloddy.* While you do this, keep the stalks of the outside leaves close up to prevent the earth from getting between the stems of the outside leaves and the inner ones; for, if it get there it checks the plant and makes the celery bad.—When you begin the *earthing* take first the *edges of the trenches;* and do not go into the middle of the intervals for the earth that you took out of the trenches. Keep working backwards, time after time, that is earthing after earthing, till you come to the earth that you dug out of the trenches; and, by this time the earth against the plants will be above the level of the land. Then you take the earth out of the middle, till, at last the earth against the plants form a *ridge* and the middle of each interval a sort of gutter. Earth up *very often,* and not put much at a time. Every week a little earth to be put up.—Thus, in October, you will have four ridges of Celery across one of the Plats, each containing 168 plants. I shall suppose one of these ridges to be wanted for use before the frost *sets in* for good. Leave another ridge to be *lock-up* by the frost, a much safer guardian than your cellar or barn-door. But, you must cover this ridge over in such a way that the *wet* will not get down into the hearts of the celery. Two-boards, a foot wide each, their edges on one side laid upon the earth of the ridge, formed into a *roof* over the point of the ridge, the upper edge of one board going an inch over the upper edge of the other; and the boards fastened well with pegs, will do the business completely; for it is not the frost, but the occasional *thaws* that you have to fear, and the *wet* and *rot* that they produce.—For the celery that is to serve from the setting in to the breaking up of the frost, you must have a bed of sand, or light earth, in a warm part of a barn, or in a cellar; and there you must lay it in, row after row, not covering the points of the leaves.—To have *seed,* take one plant, in spring, out of the ridge left in the garden. Plant it in an open place, and you will have seed enough to serve a whole township. For *soup,* the seed *bruised* is as good as the plant itself. For the number of years that the seed will keep good, see Paragraph 150.

211.

CHERVIL.

Chervil is an annual plant. Its leaves are a good deal like those of double parsley. They are used in salads. A small patch, sown in rows, like parsley, is enough.

212.

CIVES.

Cives, a little sort of onion, which is perennial. The greens only are used. A small quantity is sufficient for a garden. This plant may be propagated from seed, or from offsets.

213.

CORIANDER.

Coriander is an annual plant that some persons use in soups and salads. It is sown in spring. The seed is also used as a medicine. A small patch, probably two square yards, will be enough.

214.

CORN (INDIAN.)

To have some early, the *early sorts* must be got. A dozen or two of plants may be easily raised in pots, as directed for *Cucumbers.* See *Cucumber.*

215.

CORN-SALAD.

This is a little insignificant annual plant that some persons use in salads, though it can hardly be of any real use, where lettuce seed is to be had. It is a mere *weed*.

216.

CRESS (OR PEPPER-GRASS.)

Cress is very good in salads along with lettuces, white mustard, or rape. It should be sown in little drills, *very thick* (as should the white mustard and the rape) and cut *before it comes into rough leaf.* A small quantity, in the salad-season, should be sown every six days. This salad, as well as the mustard and the rape, may be very conveniently raised in a corner of a hot-bed made for radishes or cabbage-plants.

217.

CUCUMBER.

To give minute rules for the propagation and cultivation of this plant, in a country like this, would be waste of time. However, if you wish to have them a *month earlier* than the natural ground will bring them, do this. Make a hole, and put into it a little hot dung; let the hole be under a warm fence. Put 6 inches deep of fine rich earth on the dung. Sow a parcel of seeds in this earth; and cover at night with a bit of carpet, or sail cloth, having first fixed some hoops over this little bed.—Before the plants show the *rough* leaf, plant two into a little flower pot, and fill as many pots in this way as you please.— Have a larger bed ready to put the pots into, and covered with earth so that the pots may be plunged in the earth up to their tops. Cover this bed like the last.—When the plants have got two rough leaves out, they will begin to make a *shoot* in the middle. Pinch that shoot off.—Let them stand in this bed, till your cucumbers *sown in the natural ground come up;* then make some little holes in good rich land,

and taking a pot at a time, turn out the *ball* and fix it in the hole. These plants will bear a *month sooner* than those sown in the natural ground; and a *square* yard will contain 36 pots, and will of course, furnish plants for 36 hills of cucumbers, which, if well managed, will keep on bearing till September.—Those who have *hot-bed frames,* or *hand-lights,* will do this matter very easily.—The cucumber plant is very tender and juicy; and, therefore, when the seedlings are put into the pots, they should be *watered,* and *shaded* for a day or two; when the balls are turned into the ground, they should be *watered,* and shaded with a bough for one day. That will be enough. I have one observation to make upon the cultivation of cucumbers, melons of all sorts, and that of all the pumpkin and squash tribe; and that is, that it is a great error to sow them *too thick.* One plant in a hill is enough; and I would put *two into a pot,* merely as a bar against accidents. One will bring more weight of fruit than two (if standing near each other,) two more than three, and so on, till you come to fifty in a square foot; and then you will have no fruit at all! Let any one make the experiment, and he will find this observation mathematically true. When cucumbers are left eight or ten plants in a hill, they never shoot *strongly.* Their vines are poor and weak, the leaves become yellow, and, if they bear at all, it is poor tasteless fruit that they produce. Their bearing is over in a few weeks. Whereas, a single plant, in the same space, will send its fine green vines all around it to a great distance, and, if no fruit be left to *ripen,* will keep bearing till the white frosts come in the fall.—The roots of a cucumber will go ten feet, in fine earth, in every direction. Judge, then, how ten plants, standing close to one another, must produce mutual starvation!—If you save a cucumber for seed, let it be the *first* fine fruit that appears on the plant. The plant will cease to bear much after this fruit becomes *yellowish.*— I have said enough, under the head of *Saving Seeds,* (Paragraphs 139 to 146) to make you take care, that nothing of the melon, pumpkin or squash kind grow *near* a seed-bearing cucumber plant; and that all cucumbers of a different sort from that bearing the seed be kept at a great distance.—There are many sorts of cucumbers: the *Long Prickly,* the *Short Prickly,* the *Cluster,* and many others; but, the propagation and cultivation of all the sorts are the same.

218.

DANDELION.

This is a well-known and most wicked garden *weed,* in this country as well as in England; and I am half afraid to speak of using it as food, lest I should encourage laziness. But, there may be people without gardens, and without the means of purchasing greens in the spring; and to them what I am about to say may be of use. The Dandelion is as early as the earliest of *grass;* and, it is one of the very *best of greens,* when it is young. It is a sort of wild *Endive.* The French, who call it (from the shape of its leave) *Dent de lion,* or *Lion's tooth,* use it, *bleached,* as *salad,* and, if fine, large and well bleached, it is better than Endive, much more tender, and of a better flavour. It is very common in rich pasture land in England; and cattle and sheep, particularly the former, prefer it, as far as my observation has gone, to every other plant in the pastures. It is full of *milk*-coloured juice, and fuller of it than either the Endive or the Lettuce. In the spring (June) 1817, when I came to Long Island, and when nothing in the shape of *greens* was to be had for love or money, *Dandelions* were our resource; and I have always, since that time, looked at this *weed* with a more friendly eye.

219.

DOCK.

I have frequently mentioned the leaves of this *weed* as being sold in the market at New York. This weed and the Dandelion are the gardener's two *vegetable devils.* Nothing but absolute *burning,* or a sun that will reduce them to *powder,* will kill their roots, any little bit of which will grow, and that, too, whether lying *on,* or *in,* the ground.

Both bear seed in prodigious quantities.—The *Dock* (which is the wild *Rhubarb*) puts forth its leaves very quickly after the Dandelion; and hence it is that it is resorted to as *greens* in the spring. This is, however, a *coarse* green compared with the Dandelion. However, it is better than no greens at all after five months of winter, which has left nothing green upon the face of the earth.—If a rod or two of ground, on the south side of a wood, were trenched and made *rich*, and planted with Docks, or Dandelions, the owner, even though he had no garden, would not be in want of early greens; and, it would be better to do this than to have to go upon the *hunt* after these vegetables, which, though weeds, are not, in every place, to be found in any considerable quantity; or, at least, not without spending a good deal of time in the pursuit.—The Dock-leaf is very wholesome, as is also that of the Dandelion. They do not produce *gripings* as the greater part of the cabbage kinds are apt to do.—See *Rhubarb*.

220.

ENDIVE.

This is a salad-plant, though, like the Dandelion, it may be eaten as greens.—There are two sorts, the *curled* and the *plain,* just as there are of the Dandelion, which, as I observed before, is a sort of Endive.—The curled is *prettiest,* and is, therefore, generally preferred; but, the plain is the *best.*—Sow Endive in drills a foot apart; when the plants come up, thin them to a foot apart in the row, if they be not to be *removed* by transplantation; keep the ground clean, and hoe deep and frequently between the plants. When they get to a good size, they are to be *bleached* before they can be used as *salad;* for, while green, they are bitter and not very crisp. In order to bleach them, you must take them when *quite dry;* gather all the leaves carefully up with your hands; draw them into a conical form, and tie them round with *matting* or soft string, or little splinters of white oak. When they have remained in this state for about a fortnight, they will be bleached and fit for use.—The *time* of sowing may be as early as the weather will permit in the spring, and there may be another sowing for summer; but, it is for *winter* and spring use that Endive is most wanted; so that, the late sowings are of the most importance. Sow about the end of July, in fine rich ground. If you do not *transplant*, leave the plants at the distances before-mentioned; if you do, transplant at the same distances (a foot every way;) do it when the plants have ten leaves, and tip off both leaves and roots when you transplant. Fix the roots well as directed in the case of cabbage; and, as the plant is very juicy, and the weather hot, plant in the evening, or early in the morning, water a little, and lay some bows over to *shade* for two days, but take the bows off at night.—The best place for Endive would be the shady border. The plants will come in for use in October, November, and December. Some sown a little later must be preserved for winter use. Before the frost *sets in*, they must be tied up in a conical form, as before directed, and all *dead*, or *yellow*, leaves must be taken off. Then dig them up, with a ball of earth to each, and put them into light earth in a cellar or some warm building. Put only the roots into the earth; do not suffer the plants to touch each other; and pour a little water round the roots after you have put them in the earth. If they be *perfectly dry* when tied up, they will keep well till spring.—To have them as early as possible in the spring, sow in the *third week of August*, and do not transplant. When the *hard frost is come*, cover the whole of the ground over with straw six inches deep, and throw (if at hand) some leaves of trees over the straw, and some sticks to keep the leaves from blowing away. But, the best covering of all, in this case is, boughs of *cedar*, or of *fir*, or *laurel*; though these boughs must be, for this purpose, cut up into small parts, so that they will lie close and compact and keep out the *light*. Some ever-green boughs, and some leaves of trees thrown over them, form, perhaps, the best covering in the world for plants of this description. But, observe; you must let the *frost come*. The ground must be right hard when you put the covering on; or else, the plants will rot. They must see the sun no more till spring.—When the frost *breaks up*, take off the covering; hoe the ground as soon as dry, and proceed to perfect the plants in the manner before described.—One of these plants will produce *seed* enough to last you for five years.—There need not be many of these plants. *Lettuces* are their rivals, and are a great deal better.—I have mentioned *matting* in this article, as a thing to *tie* with. This matting is nothing more than the *threads* of those large things, in which foreign goods sometimes come packed up. These things are in England called *Mats*, and the threads of which they are composed, are by gardeners, called *matting*. The gardeners use this for ties to Espalier trees; they tie on their *grafts* with it; they tie up their flowers with it; and, in short, it is the *string* of the gardeners. The Mats, thousands of bales of which are imported into England from Russia, are used to cover the hot-beds with, and for various other purposes.—But, *matting* is to be had, and with very little trouble, without sending to Russia for it. Any one who has a *spare tree* may have plenty of matting. When I came to Long Island, I cut down a chestnut, of about a foot diameter, and that furnished me with a store of matting ties. The tree was cut in June; the outer bark taken off; and then the *inner*-bark came off in long *flakes*, some broad and some narrow, the whole length of the clear trunk, which was about 15 feet. I just hung this up to dry; and that was *matting*, to be cut into any length, and ready to use for any tie, where much strength was not required. The only precautions are: keep the matting in the dry, and when you use it *dip it in water* first for a few minutes, and take it out of the water as you use it. If you have put more into the water than you want for that time, take it out and hang it up in the dry again; and it will receive no injury.

221.

FENNEL.

Fennel is a *perennial* plant; propagated from *seed*, or from offsets; and sown, or planted, either in spring or fall. The plants should stand about a foot asunder. It is a tall plant with *hairy* leaves. Its leaves are used in salads, are chopped up fine to put in melted butter eaten with fish; they are boiled with fish to give the fish a flavour, and, they are tied round *mackerel,* particularly, when these are broiled. The French, who excel in the cooking of fish, always do this. The leaves, thus broiled, become crisp; and, they are then of a very fine flavour. In winter, the seed, bruised, gives fish the same flavour as the leaves do in summer; and, to my taste, butter, seasoned with *Fennel,* is better than any of the fish sauces, bought at the shops.—It is a very hardy plant. Two yards square will contain enough for any family; and, once in the ground, it will stand there for an age, or ten ages, as far as I know.

222.

GARLICK.

Almost all nations except the English, the Americans, and the French, make great and constant use of Garlick; and, even the French use it, frequently, to an extent that would drive us from the table.—It is propagated from seed, or from offsets: and is sown, or planted, either in spring or fall. For winter-use, the roots are taken up and kept in the dry, as onions are.

223.

GOURD.

I do not know any use that it is of. See *Pumpkin.*

224.

HOP.

To range the Hop amongst *Vegetables* may appear odd; but, it is a *garden-plant* in America, and does give you, if you like to have it, a very good dish for the table. It is wanted to produce its fruit for the making of *yeast,* or *beer,* or both; and, to get good hops, there should be some cultivation. Any bit of a root will grow and become a plant. The young plants should be planted in the fall, three or four together in a clump, or hill, and the hills should be from seven to ten feet apart. The first year of planting, put four rods, or little poles, to each hill, and let two vines go up each pole, treading the rest of the vines down to creep about the ground. In a month after the vines begin to mount the poles, cut off all the creeping vines; and draw up a hill of earth against the poles all round, and cover all the crowns of the plants. In short, make a hill a foot high with a flattish top, and then fork up the ground between the hills and break it fine. When weeds begin to appear, *hoe* the ground clean; and, at the end of another month draw some more earth up, and make the hill bigger and higher.—When the fall comes, cut off the vines that have gone up the pole a foot from the ground; take down the poles; dig down the hills, and, with a corn-hoe, open the ground all round the crowns of the plants; and, before winter sets in, cut all close down to the very crowns, and then cover the crowns over with earth three or four inches thick. Through this earth the hop-shoots will start in the spring. You will want but eight of them to go up your four poles; and the rest, when three inches long, you may cut, and eat as *asparagus;* cook them in the same manner, and you will find them a very *delightful vegetable.*—This year you put poles 20 feet long to your hops. Proceed the same as before, only make the *hills larger;* and this year you will have plenty of hops to gather for use.—The next, and every succeeding year, you may put poles 40 or 50 feet long; but they must not be *too large at bottom.* Be sure to open the ground every fall, and to cut all off close down to the *crown of the plants,* which, when pared off with a sharp knife, will look like a piece of *cork.*—In England, where there are more hops used than in all the rest of the world, it requires *four or five years* to bring a hop hill to perfection. Even then, a pole from 15 to 20 feet long is generally long enough; and the crop of *thirty hills* is, upon an average, not more than equal to that of *one hill* in the hop-plantations on the Susquehannah; notwithstanding that, on the Susquehannah, they merely plough the ground in spring; never open the crowns and pare them down, leave the loose creeping vines together with the weeds and grass to be eaten, in summer, by *sheep*, which also eat the leaves of the mounting vines as far as they, by putting their fore feet against the poles, can reach up; and yet, in England, the Hop-lands are called hop-*gardens*, and are cultivated and kept in a garden state.—But, hops are to be *preserved*. They are fit to gather, when you see, upon opening the leaves of the hop, a good deal of *yellow dust*, and when the seeds, which you will find at the sockets of the leaves of the hop, begin to be plump.—Gather them nicely, and let no leaves or stalks be amongst them; and lay them out on a cloth to dry in the sun, taking care that no rain fall upon them, and that they be not out in the dew.—When *perfectly dry*, put them, very hardly and closely pressed, into a new bag, made of thick Russia linen, such as they make strong trowsers of. And, in this state, they will, if necessary, keep good and fit for use (if kept in a dry place) for *twenty years*, or, perhaps, three times twenty. I have used hops, for brewing, at *ten years old*, and found them just as *efficient* as new hops of the same original quality. However, *people say* that the fresh hops have a more *lively flavour*; and, as any *stick* will, in America, carry enough to supply a family with hops for the making of *yeast-cakes*, it must be shocking laziness not to put a few by every year.

225.

HORSE-RADISH.

Like every other plant, this bears *seed;* but it is best propagated by cutting bits of its roots into lengths of two inches, and putting them, spring or fall, into the ground about a foot deep with a setting stick. They will find their way up the first year; and the second they will be fine large roots, if the ground be trenched deeply and made pretty good. Half a square perch of ground, planted at a foot apart every way, will, if kept clear of weeds, produce enough for a family that eats roast-beef every day of their lives. You must take care that the Horse-radish roots do not spread, and that bits of them be not flung about the ground; for, when once in, no *tillage* will get them out. They must be, like the Dock and Dandelion roots, absolutely burnt by *fire*, or by a sun that will reduce them to a state of a dry stick; or must be taken up and *carried away* from the spot. Though a very valuable and wholesome article of diet, it is a most *pernicious weed*.

226.

HYSSOP.

Hyssop is a sort of shrub, the flower-spikes of which are used, fresh or dried, for medicinal purposes. It is propagated from seed, or from offsets. A very little of it is enough for any garden.

227.

JERUSALEM ARTICHOKE.

This plant bears at the root, like a potatoe, which, to the great degradation of many of the human race, is every where well known. But, this Artichoke, which is also dug up and cooked like a potatoe, has, at any rate, the merit of giving no trouble either in the propagation or the cultivation. A handful of the bits of its fruit, or even of its roots, flung about a piece of ground of any sort, will keep bearing for ever, in spite of grass and of weeds; the difficulty being, not to get it to grow, but to get the ground free from it, when once it has taken to growing. It is a very poor, insipid vegetable; but, if you wish to have it, now and then, the best way is to keep it out of the garden; and to dig up the corner of some *field*, and throw some *seed* or some roots into it.

228.

LAVENDER.

A beautiful little well known shrub of uses equally well known. Hundreds of acres are cultivated in England for the flowers to be used in distillation. It may be propagated from seed; but is easiest propagated from slips, taken off in the spring, and planted in good moist ground in the shade. When planted out it should be in rows three feet apart and two feet apart in the rows. If the flowers be to be preserved, the flower-stalks should be cut off before the blossoms begin to fade at all.

229.

LEEK.

There are two sorts; the *narrow-leaved,* and the *flag-leek,* the latter of which is by much the best—Some people like leeks better than onions; and they are better in soup.—Sow in the fall, or, as early in the spring as you can.—About four yards square is enough. Put the rows eight inches asunder, and thin the plants to three inches apart in the row. Hoe deeply and frequently between the plants till the middle of July, and then take the plants up, cut their roots off to an inch long, and cut off the leaves also a good way down. Make trenches, like those for *Celery* (which see,) only not more than *half as deep,* and *half as wide apart.* Manure the trenches with rotten dung, or other rich manure. Put in the plants as you do the Celery plants, and plant about five inches asunder. As the Leeks grow, *earth them up* by degrees like Celery; and, at last, you will have Leeks 18 inches long under ground, and as thick as your wrist. One of these is worth a dozen of poor little hard things. If you have a *row* across one of the Plats it will be plenty, perhaps. Such row will contain about a *hundred and sixty.* One third may be used, perhaps, before the winter sets in: another third taken up and put by for winter, in precisely the same way that Celery is; the other third, covered in the same way that Celery is, will be ready for spring use.—See *Celery.*— Three Leeks planted out for seed, will ripen their seed in August, and will give you seed enough for the *next year,* and some to give to five or six neighbours.

230.

LETTUCE.

This great article of the garden is milky, refreshing, and pleasanter to a majority of tastes than any other plant, the Asparagus hardly excepted. So necessary is it as the principal ingredient of a *good salad,* that it is, both in France and England, called "salad" by great numbers of people. It is good in *stews;* good boiled with *green-peas;* and, even as a dish boiled as cabbage is, it is an excellent vegetable. Yet, I never saw a really fine Lettuce in America. The obstacles are, the complete impossibility of preserving plants of the *fine* sorts in the natural ground during the winter; and the *great heat,* which will not suffer those sorts to *loave,* if they be sowed in the natural ground in the spring.—The *hardy* sorts are the *green cabbage-lettuce* (or *hardy green,*) and the *brown-cabbage.* These are *flat* plants. Their outside leaves spread forth upon the ground, and they curl into a sort of loaf in the centre. The plants of *these* may be preserved through the winter in the natural ground, in the manner directed for *Endive plants,* (which see under *Endive*) and may be sowed at the same time for that purpose. But these are very poor things. They have, though bleached at the heart, a slimy feel in the mouth; and are not *crisp* and refreshing. There are, I believe, twenty sorts, two of which only it will be enough to mention, *green-coss* and *white-coss,* the former of which is of a darker green than the latter, is rather hardier, and *not quite so good.* These, when true to their kind and in a proper situation, rise up, and fold in their leaves to a solid loaf, like a sugar-loaf cabbage, and, in rich land, with good management, they will become nearly as large. When you cut one of these from the stem, and pull off its outside leaves, you have a large *lump of white* enough for a salad for ten people, unless they be French, and, then you must have a lettuce to every person. Every body knows how to sow lettuce-seed along a drill, in the spring, to let the plants stand as thick as grass, and to cut it along with a knife, and gather it up by handfuls. But, this is not *lettuce.* It is *herbage,* and really fit only for pigs and cows. It is a raw, green, Dandelion, and is not quite so good.—The plants of these fine sorts may, indeed, be kept through the winter in the same manner, and with the same care, as Cauliflower plants (which see in Paragraph 209;) but, if this be not done, you must raise them in the spring in precisely the same way as the very earliest cabbage-plants, for which see Paragraphs from 77 to 94.—Put the plants out into the natural ground, about a fortnight before the general Corn-planting time. Do not put them in a place *full to the sun;* but in the east borders, or in the west border. Make the ground *rich, right strong,* break it well, and, in transplanting, keep as much earth as you can about the roots, and give a little water; and transplant *in the evening.*—These plants will *loave* about the time of the early cabbages, and some of them will not go off to seed for six weeks after they are loaved. So that, about two square feet of a hot-bed will give you a great quantity of *real* lettuces.—Let one plant (a very fine one) stand for *seed;* and it will give you plenty of seed for a year or two.—Whenever you transplant Lettuces, give them a little water, and, if it be a small bed, *shade* them a little. If you sow in the natural ground in the spring, be sure to transplant into the shady borders.—And be sure always to make the ground *rich* for these fine Lettuces.

231.

MANGEL-WURZEL.

This may be called *Cattle-beet.* Some persons plant it in gardens. It is a *coarse* Beet, and is cultivated and preserved as the Beet is.

232.

MARJORAM.

One sort is *annual* and one *perennial.* The former is called *summer* and the latter *winter.* The first sown as early as possible in the spring; and, the latter propagated by *offsets;* that is, by parting the roots. The plants may stand pretty close. As the winter sort cannot be *got at* in winter, some of both ought to be preserved by *drying.* Cut it *just before it comes out into bloom,* hang it up in little bunches to dry, first, for a day, in the sun; then in the shade; and, when quite dry, put it in paper bags, tied up, and the bags hung up in a dry place.

233.

MARIGOLD.

An ANNUAL plant. Sow the seed, spring or fall; when the bloom is at full, gather the flowers; pull the leaves of the flower out of their sockets; lay them on paper to dry, in the *shade*. When dry put them into paper bags. They are excellent in broths and soups and stews. Two square yards planted with Marigolds will be sufficient. It is the *single* Marigold that ought to be cultivated for culinary purposes. The *double* one is an *ornamental* flower, and a very mean one indeed.

234.

MELON.

There are, all the world knows, two distinct tribes: the *Musk,* and the *Water.* Of the former, the sorts are endless, and, indeed, of the latter also. Some of both tribes are *globular* and others *oblong;* and, in both tribes there are different colours, as well with regard to flesh as to rind.—In this fine country, where they all come to perfection in the natural ground, no distinction is made as to *earliness,* or *lateness* in sorts; and, in other respects, some like one sort best and some another. Amongst the Musk melons, the *Citron* is, according to my taste, the finest by far; and the finest Water melons that I have ever tasted were raised from seed that came out of melons grown in Georgia.—As to the manner of propagating, cultivating, and sowing the seed of melons, see *Cucumber,* and only observe, that all that is there said applies to melons as well as to cucumbers. To have melons a *month earlier* than the natural ground sowings will produce them is an object of much greater importance than to have cucumbers so much earlier; and, to accomplish that object, you have only to use the same means, in every respect, that I have described for the getting of early cucumbers. The soil should be *rich* for melons; but it ought not to be *freshly* dunged; for that is apt to *rot* the plants, especially in a wet year. They like a light and rather sandy soil, and, any where near the sea, wood ashes, or sopers' ashes, is, probably, the best manure, and especially in dry-bottomed land; for ashes *attract* and *retain* the moisture of the atmosphere. It is a great mistake to suppose, that ashes are of a *burning* quality. They always produce the most and best effect in *dry bottomed* land.—Melons should be *cultivated* well. You should leave but *one plant in a hill;* and should till the ground between the plants, while they are growing, until it be covered by the vines. If the plants stand too close, the vines will be weak, and fruit small, thick-rinded, and poor as to flavour.

235.

MINT.

There are two sorts; one is of a darker green than the other: the former is called *pepper-mint,* and is generally used for *distilling* to make mint water: the latter, which is called *spearmint,* is used for the table, in many ways. The French snip a little into their *salads;* we boil a bunch amongst green peas, to which it gives a pleasant flavour; chopped up small, and put, along with sugar, into vinegar, we use it as sauce for *roasted lamb;* and a very pleasant sauce it is.— Mint *may* be propagated from seed; but, a few bits of its roots will spread into a bed in a year.—To have it in winter, preserve it precisely like Marjoram (which see,) and, instead of *chopping* it for sauce, crumble it between your fingers.

236.

MUSTARD.

There is a *white seeded* sort and a *brown seeded.* The *white* mustard is used in *salads* along with the Cress, or *Pepper-Grass,* and is sown and cultivated in the same way. (See Cress.) The *brown* is that which table-mustard is made of.—It is sown in rows, two feet apart, early in the spring. The plants ought to be thinned to four or five inches apart. Good tillage between the rows. The seed will be ripe in July, and then the stalks should be cut off, and, when quite dry, the seed threshed out, and put by for use.—Why should any man that has a garden *buy* mustard? Why should he want the English to send him out, in a bottle, and sell him for a quarter of a dollar, less and worse mustard than he can raise in his garden for a penny? The English mustard is, in general, a thing *fabricated,* and is as false as the *glazed* and *pasted* goods, sent out by the fraudulent fabricators of Manchester. It is a composition of *baked bones* reduced to powder, some *wheat flour,* some *colouring,* and a *drug* of some sort that gives the pungent taste. Whoever uses that mustard *freely* will find a *burning in his inside long after he has swallowed the mustard.* Why should any man, who has a garden, *buy* this poisonous stuff? The mustard-seed *ground in a little mustard mill* is what he ought to use. He will have *bran* and all; and his mustard will not look yellow like the English composition; but, we do not object to Rye-bread on account of its *colour*! Ten pounds of seed will grow upon a perch of ground; and ten pounds of mustard is more than any man can want in a year. The plants do not occupy the ground more than fourteen weeks, and may be followed by another crop of any plant, and even of mustard if you like. This, therefore, is a very useful plant, and ought to be cultivated by every farmer, and every man who has a garden.

237.

NASTURTIUM.

An annual plant, with a half-red half-yellow flower, which has an offensive smell; but, it bears a seed enveloped in a fleshy pod, and that pod, taken before the seed becomes ripe, is used as a thing to *pickle.*—The seeds should be sown in the fall, or very early in the spring. The plants should have pretty long bushy sticks put to them; and four or five of them will bear a great quantity of pods.—They will grow in almost any ground; but, the better the ground the fewer of them are necessary.

238.

ONION.

This is one of the main vegetables. Its uses are many, and they are all well known. The modes of cultivation for crop are various.

Three I shall mention, and by either a good crop may be raised.— Sow in the fall (See Paragraph 159,) or early in the Spring. Let the ground be *rich,* but not from *fresh dung.* Make the ground very *fine;* make the rows a foot apart, and scatter the seed *thinly* along a drill two inches deep. Then fill in the drills; and then press the earth down upon the seed by *treading the ground all over.* Then give the ground a *very slight* smoothing over with a rake.—When the plants get to be three inches high, thin them to four inches, or to eight inches if you wish to have very large onions.—Keep the ground clear of weeds by *hoeing;* but, do not *hoe deep,* nor *raise earth* about the plants; for these make them run to *neck* and not to *bulk.*—When the tips of the leaves begin to be brown, bend down the necks, so that the leaves lie flat with the ground. When the leaves are nearly dead, pull up the onions, and lay them to dry, in order to be put away for winter use.—Some persons, instead of sowing the onions *all along* the drill drop four or five seeds at every six or seven inches distance; and leave the onions to grow thus, *in clumps;* and this is not a bad way; for, they will *squeeze each other out.* They will not be *large;* but, they will be ripe *earlier,* and will not run to neck.—The third mode of cultivation is as follows: sow the onions any time between April and the middle of June, in drills *six* inches apart, and put the seed *very thick* along the drills. Let all the plants stand, and they will get to be about as big round as the top of your little finger. Then the leaves will get yellow, and, when that is the case, pull up the onions and lay them on a board, till the sun have withered up the leaves. Then take these diminutive onions, put them in a bag, and hang them up in a dry place till spring. As soon as the frost is gone, and the ground dry, plant out these onions in good and fine ground, in rows a foot apart. Make, *not drills,* but little marks along the ground; and put the onions at six or eight inches apart. Do not cover them with the earth; but just *press them down upon* the mark with your thumb and forefinger. The ground ought to be trodden and slightly raked again before you make the *marks;* for *no earth should rise up,* about the plants.—Proceed after this as with sown onions; only observe, that, if any should be *running up to seed,* you must *twist down the neck* as soon as you perceive it. But, observe this: the *shorter* the time that these onions have been in the ground the year before, the *less likely will they be to run to seed.*—Preserving onions is an easy matter. Frost never hurts them, *unless you move them during the time that they are frozen.* Any dry, airy place, will, therefore, do. They should not be kept in a *warm* place; for they will *heat* and grow. The neatest way is to tie them up in ropes; that is to say, to tie them round sticks, or straight straw, with *matting* (See *Endive.*)—For seed, pick out the *finest onions,* and plant them out in rich land, in the spring.—To grow this seed upon a large scale, plough the land into four feet ridges, lay plenty of dung along the furrows, plough the ground back over the dung, flatten the top of the ridge a little, and put along, on the top of the ridge *two rows* of onions, the rows seven inches apart, and the onions, seven inches apart in the rows. When the weeds come, hoe the *tops* of the ridges with a small *hoe,* and plough first from and then to the ridges, two or three times, at the distance of two or three weeks, as in the case of *Ruta Baga,* culti-vated in the *field.*—When the seed is ripe, cut off the heads and col-lect them in such a way as not to scatter the seed. Lay them on cloths, in the sun, till dry as dust; and then thresh out the seed, win-now it, and put it away. The seed will be dead ripe in August, and transplanted Ruta Baga, or Early York Cabbages, or even Kidney dwarf beans, or, perhaps, Buckwheat, may follow upon the same ground, the same year.—In a *garden* there always ought to be a crop to succeed seed-onions the same summer.

239.

PARSLEY.

Known to every human being to bear its seed the second year, and, after that, to die away. It may be sown at *any season* when the frost is out of the ground. The best way is to sow it in spring, and in very *clean* ground; because the seed lies long in the ground, and, if the ground be foul, the weeds choak the plants at their coming up.—A bed of six feet long and four wide, the seed sown in drills at eight inches apart, is enough for any family in the world.—But, every body *likes parsley*, and where the winter is so long and so sharp as it is in this country, the main thing is to be able to *keep parsley through the winter*. It can not be preserved *dry*, with success, like *Mint, Marjoram*, and the rest of the pot-herbs. It is possible to preserve it *green*, because I have done it; but, it loses its *smell* and flavour. Therefore, to have Parsley in winter, you must keep it *alive*. If you have a Green-house (or you may do it even in any of the window seats of a house) half a dozen flower-pots, planted with stout plants in September, and taken into the house in November, will be sufficient. As soon as winter breaks up, put them out in the natural ground; and thus you have plenty of Parsley all the year round. However, Parsley may be preserved in the natural ground. You have only to put straw, or leaves of trees, or long litter, six inches thick on the bed, and to lay on something to prevent the covering from being blown off. (See, *Endive*.) This will preserve its leaves from being destroyed; and, when you go to get it, you must lift up the covering, of a part of the bed, and put it down again.

240.

PARSNIP.

As to season of sowing, sort of land, preparation of ground, distances, and cultivation and tillage, precisely the same as the *Carrot*, which see, Paragraph 208. But, as to preservation during winter, and for *spring use*, the Parsnip stands all frost without injury, and even with benefit. So that, all you want is to put up for winter as many as you want during the hard frost; and these you may put up in the same manner as directed for Carrots and Beets.—The greens of Parsnips are as good for cow feed as those of Carrots; but, if the Parsnips be to stand out in the ground all the winter, the greens should not be cut off in the fall.

241.

PEA.

This is one of those vegetables which all men most like. Its culture is universal, where people have the means of growing it. The *sorts* of peas are very numerous; and I will mention a few of them presently.—The soil should be *good,* and *fresh dung* is good manure for them. Ashes; and compost, very good; but peas, like Indian Corn, will bear to be actually sown upon dung. Never were finer peas grown than there are grown in the United States; and, as we shall presently see, they *may* be had, in the open ground, in Long Island, from first of June till the *sharp* frosts set in.—The sorts are numerous, one class is of a *small* size and the other *large.* The latter grow *taller,* and are longer in coming to perfection, than the former. The earliest of all is the little white pea, called, in Long Island, the *May-Pea,* and, in England, the *early frame-pea.* Then come the *early Charleton,* the *Hotspur,* the *Blue Pea,* the *Dwarf* and *Tall Marrowfats;* and several others, especially the *Knight Pea,* the seed of which is rough, uneven shaped and shrivelled, and the plant of which grows *very tall.*—All the sorts may be grown in America, *without sticks,* and even better than with. I have this year (1819) the finest peas I ever saw, and the crop the most abundant. And this is the manner, in which I have sown and cultivated them. I ploughed the ground into ridges, the tops of which (for the dwarf sorts) were four feet apart. I then put a good parcel of yard-dung into the furrows; and ploughed the earth back upon the dung. I then levelled the top of the ridge a little, and drew two drills along upon it at six inches distant from each other. In these I sowed the peas. When the peas were about three inches high, I hoed the ground deep and well between the rows and on each outside of them. I then ploughed the ground from them, and to them again, in the same way as in the case of Swedish Turnips. In a week or two afterwards they had another ploughing; and soon after this they fell, and *lay down the sides of the ridges.* This was the way in which I managed all the sorts, only in the case of the *Knight Pea* I put the ridges at six feet asunder.—This was, of every sort, the very finest crop of peas I ever saw in my life. When not sticked, and sown upon level ground, peas fall about *irregularly*, and, in case of much wet, the under pods rot; but, from the ridges they fall regularly, and the wet does not lodge about them. You walk up the furrows to gather the peas; and nothing can be more beautiful, or more convenient. The culture in the garden may be the same, except that the work which is done with the *plough* in the field, must, in the garden, be done with the *spade*.—As to seasons, the early pea may be sown *in the fall*. See Paragraph 159. But, in this case, care must be taken to guard against *mice*. Sow about four inches deep, and tread the ground well down. When the frost *sets in*, all is safe till winter breaks up. These peas will be earlier by ten or fifteen days than any that you can sow in the spring.—If you sow in the spring, do it as soon as the ground is dry enough to go upon. Sow the May Pea, some Charletons, some Hotspurs, some Blue Peas, some Marrowfats, and some Knight Pea, all at the same time, and they will come one after another, so as to give you green peas till nearly August. In June (about the middle) sow some early pea again and also some Marrowfats and Knight Pea; and these will give you peas till September. Sow some of each sort middle of August, and they will give you green peas till the *hardish* frosts come.—But, these two last sowings (June and August) ought to be under the *South* fence, so as to get as much *coolness* as possible.

242.

PENNYROYAL.

A medicinal herb. It is perennial. A little patch, a foot square, is enough.

243.

PEPPER.

See *Capsicum*.

244.

PEPPER GRASS.

See *Cress*.

245.

POTATOE.

Every body knows how to cultivate this plant; and, as to its *preservation* during winter, if you can ascertain the degree of warmth necessary to keep a *baby* from perishing, you know precisely the precautions required to preserve a potatoe.—As to sorts, they are as numerous as the stones of a pavement in a large city; but, there is one sort earlier than all others. It is a small, round, white potatoe, that has *no blossom,* and the leaf of which is of a pale green, very thin, very smooth, and nearly of the shape and size of the inside of a *lemon* cut asunder longways. This potatoe, if planted with other sorts in the spring, will be ripe *six weeks* sooner than any other sort. I have had *two crops* of this potatoe ripen on the same ground in the same year, in England, the second crop from potatoes of the first. Two crops could be raised in America with the greatest facility.— But, if you once get this sort, and wish to keep it, you must take care that no other sort grow *with* it, or near it; for, potatoes of this kind mix the breed more readily than any thing else, though they have no *bloom!* If some plants of this blossomless kind grow with or near the other kinds, they will produce plants with a rough leaf, some of them will even *blow,* and they will *lose their quality of earliness.* This is quite enough to prove the fallacy of the doctrine of a communication of the *farina* of the flowers of plants.

246.

POTATOE (SWEET.)

This plant is cultivated in much the same way as the last. *Heat* is what it chiefly wants; and great care indeed must be taken to preserve it in winter.

247.

PUMPKIN.

See *Cucumber.* The cultivation is the same, and every body knows the different qualities of the different sorts, and how to preserve and use them all.

248.

PURSLANE.

A mischievous weed that Frenchmen and pigs eat when they can get nothing else. Both use it in salad, that is to say, raw.

249.

RADISH.

A great variety of sorts. Sown *thin* in little drills six inches asunder. Sown as early as possible in the spring, and a little bed every three weeks all summer long. The early scarlet is the best. Radishes may be raised early in a hot-bed precisely as cabbage-plants are.

250.

RAMPION.

This is the smallest seed of which we have any knowledge. A thimble full, properly distributed, would sow an acre of land. It is sown in the spring, in very fine earth. Its roots are used in soups and salads. Its leaves are also used in salads. A yard square is enough for any garden.

251.

RAPE.

This is a *field-plant* for sheep; but it is very good to sow like *White Mustard,* to use as salad, and it is sown and raised in the same way.

252.

RHUBARB.

This is one of the capital articles of the garden, though I have neven seen it in America. The *Dock* is the wild Rhubarb, and if you look at, and *taste*, the *root*, you will see the proof of it. The Rhubarb plant has leaves as broad and long as those of the *burrdock*. Its comes forth, like the dock, very early in the spring. When its leaves are pretty large, you cut them off close to the stem, and, if the plant be fine, the *stalk of the leaf* will be from eight inches to a foot long. You peel the outside skin from these *stalks*, and then cut the stalks up into bits about as big as the first joint of a lady's third finger. You put these into puddings, pies, tarts, just as you would green goose-berries and green currants, and some people think they are better than either: at any rate, they are full *six weeks earlier.*—The plant, like the dock, is *hardy*, is raised from *seed*, from the *roots*, will grow in any ground, though best in rich ground; and the same plants will last for an age. It is a very valuable plant, and no garden ought to be without it. I should think, that a hundred wagon-loads of the stalks are yearly sold in London. A bunch which you can clasp with your two hands sells for a shilling or two in the very early part of the season: and that is nearly half a dollar. This circumstance sufficiently speaks its praise.

253.

ROSEMARY.

Rosemary is a beautiful little shrub. One of them may be enough in a garden. It is propagated from *slips*, taken off in the spring and planted in a cool place.

254.

RUE.

Still more beautiful. Propagated in the same manner. One plant of the kind is enough.

255.

RUTABAGA.

See *Turnip*.

256.

SAGE.

Sage is raised from seed, or from slips. To have it at hand for winter it is necessary to *dry it;* and it ought to be cut, for this purpose, *before it comes out into bloom,* as, indeed, is the case with *all other herbs.*

257.

SALSAFY.

Salsafy, called, by some, *oyster plant,* is good in soups, or to eat like the *parsnip.* It is cultivated like the parsnip, and, like it, stands out the whole of an American winter.

258.

SAMPHIRE.

Samphire is propagated from seed, or from offsets. It is perennial, and is sometimes used as a pickle, or in salads.

259.

SAVORY.

Two sorts, *summer* and *winter.* The former is annual, and the latter perennial.

260.

SAVOY.

See *Cabbage,* Paragraph 201.

261.

SCORZENERA.

This is only another kind of SALSAFY. It is cultivated and used in the same manner as Salsafy is.

262.

SHALOT.

A little sort of Onion, which is taken up in the fall and kept for winter use. Each plant multiplies itself in the summer by adding offsets all round it. One of them is a plant to put out in the spring to produce other offsets for use and for planting out again. They should be planted in rows six inches apart, and four inches apart in the rows. The ground should not be wet at bottom, and should be kept very clean during the summer.

263.

SKIRRET.

Skirret is cultivated for its root, which is used in soups. It may be raised from seed, or from offsets. It is perennial, and a very small patch may suffice.

264.

SORREL.

This is no other than the wild sorrel cultivated. It is propagated from seed, or from offsets. It is perennial. The French make large messes of it; but a foot square may suffice for an American garden.

265.

SPINACH.

Every one knows how good and useful a plant this is. It is certainly preferable to any of the cabbage kind in point of wholesomeness, and it is of very easy cultivation. There is, in fact, but *one sort,* that I know any thing of, though the seed is sometimes more *prickly* than at other times. To have spinach very early in the spring, sow (Long Island) on or about the first week of September, in drills a foot apart, and, when the plants are well up, thin them to six inches. They will be fine and strong by the time that the winter *sets in;* and, as soon as that time comes, cover them over well with straw, and keep the straw on till the breaking up of the frost.—Sow more as soon as the frost is out of the ground; and this will be in perfection in June.—You may sow again in May; but the plants will go off to seed before they attain too much size.—If you save seed, save it from plants that have stood the winter.

266.

SQUASH.

Squash is, in all its varieties, cultivated like the *Cucumber*, which see.

267.

TANSY.

Tansy, a perennial culinary and medicinal herb, propagated from seed, or offsets. One root in a garden is enough.

268.

TARRAGON.

Tarragon is a very hot, peppery herb. It is used in soup and salads. It is perennial, and may be propagated from seed, or from offsets, or slips, put out in spring. Its young and tender tops only are used. It is eaten with beef-steaks in company with minced shalots. A man may live very well without it; but, an Englishman once told me, that he and six others once eat some beef-steaks with Shalots and Tarragon, and that "they voted unanimously, that beef-steaks never were so eaten!" It must be dried, like *mint*, for winter use.

269.

THYME.

There are two distinct sorts. Both are perennial, and both may be propagated either from seed, or from offsets.

270.

TOMATUM.

This plant comes from the countries bordering on the Mediterranean. In England it requires to be raised in artificial heat, and to be planted out against warm walls. *Here* it would require neither. It climbs up very high, and would require bushy sticks. It bears a sort of apple about as big as a black walnut with its green husk on. This fruit is used to thicken stews and soups, and great quantities are sold in London. It is raised from seed only, being an annual; and the seed should be sown at a great distance, seeing that the plants occupy a good deal of room.

271.

TURNIP.

It is useless to attempt to raise them by sowing in the spring: they are never good till the fall.—The sorts of Turnips are numerous, but, for a *garden*, it is quite sufficient to notice *three;* the *early white,* the *flat yellow,* and the *Swedish,* or *Rutabaga,* which last is a very different plant indeed from the other two.—The two former sorts should be sown about the end of July, in rows (in a garden) two feet apart, and thinned out to a foot distance in the rows. Good and deep hoeing and one digging should take place during their growth; for, a large turnip of the same age is better, weight for weight, than a small one, just as the largest apples, or peaches, growing upon the same tree, are better than the small ones growing on it the same year.—The *Swedish* turnip, so generally preferred for table use here, and so seldom used for the table in England, ought to be sown *early in June,* in rows at a foot apart and thinned to three inches in the rows. About the middle of July they ought to be transplanted upon ridges three feet apart (in a *garden,*) and during their growth, ought to be kept clean, and to be dug between twice at least, as deep as a good spade can be made to go.—As to the preserving of turnips during the winter, follow precisely the directions given for the preserving of *Beets*. See *Beet*.—But the Swedish Turnip is of further use as producing most excellent *greens* in the spring, and at a very early season. To draw this benefit from them, the best way is, to leave a row or two in the ground, and, when the winter is about to *set in*, cover them all over with straw or cedar boughs. Take these off when the winter breaks up, and you will have very early and most excellent greens; and, when you have done with the greens, the Turnips are very good to eat.

272.

WORMWOOD.

Wormwood is an herb purely medicinal. It may be propagated from seed, from slips, or from offsets. It ought not to occupy a space of more than a foot square. It must be dried and put by in bags for winter use.

V

Fruits.

Propagation, Planting, Cultivation.

PROPAGATION.
273.

All the Fruits to be treated of here, except the *Strawberry*, are the produce of *trees* or of *woody plants*. All these may be propagated from *seed*, and some are so propagated. But others are usually propagated by *cuttings, slips, layers*, or *suckers:* or by *budding* or *grafting* upon *stocks*.

274.

The methods of propagation, best suited to each kind, will be mentioned under the *name* of the kinds respectively; and, therefore, in this place I am to describe the several methods generally, and the management suited to each.

275.

When the propagation is from *seed*, the sowing should be in *good ground*, finely broken, and the seed should by no means be sown too thick. How to save and preserve the seed will be spoken of under the names of the several trees. But, the seed being *good*, it should be well sown, well covered, and carefully preserved from mice and other vermin.

276.

CUTTINGS.

Cuttings are short pieces, cut in the spring, from shoots of the *last year,* and it is, in most cases, best, if they have a joint or two of the *former year's wood,* at the bottom of them. The *cutting* should have altogether, about six joints, or buds; and three of these should be under ground when planted. The cuts should be performed with a *sharp knife,* so that there may be nothing ragged or bruised about either wood or bark. The time for taking off cuttings is that of the breaking up of the frost. They should be planted in a *shady place,* and watered with rain water, in dry weather, until they have got shoots several inches long. When they have such shoots they have *roots,* and when they have these, no more watering is necessary. Besides these occasional waterings, the ground should, especially in hot countries, be covered with leaves of trees, or muck, or something that will keep the ground cool during the hot and dry weather.

277.

SLIPS.

Slips differ from cuttings in this, that the former are not *cut,* but *pulled,* from the tree. You take a shoot of the *last year,* and pull it downwards, and thus slip it off. You trim the ragged back off; then shorten the shoot so that it have six joints left; and then plant it and manage it in the same manner as directed for cuttings. The season for the work is also the same.

278.

LAYERS.

You take a limb, or branch of a tree, in the fall, or early in Spring, and pull it down in such a way as to cause its top, or small shoots and twigs to lie upon the ground. Then *fasten* the limb down by a peg or two, so that its own force will not raise it up. Then prune off all the small branches and shoots that stick upright, and, having a parcel of shoots lying horizontally, *lay* earth upon the whole, all along upon the limb from the point where it begins to touch the ground, and also upon all the *bottoms of all the shoots*. Then cut the shoots off at the points, leaving only two or three joints or buds beyond the earth. The earth, laid on should be *good*, and the ground should be fresh-digged and made very fine and smooth before the branches be laid upon it. The earth, laid on, should be from six inches to a foot thick. If the limb, or mother branch, be very *stubborn*, a little cut on the lower side of it will make it the more easy to be held down. The ground should be kept clean from weeds, and as *cool* as possible in hot weather. Perhaps rocks or stones (not large) are the best and coolest covering. These layers will be ready to take up and plant out as trees after they have been laid *a year*.

279.

SUCKERS.

Suckers are, in general, but poor things, whether in the forest, or in the fruit garden. They are shoots that come up *from the roots*, at a distance from the stem of the tree, or, at least, they do not come out of that stem. They run to wood and to suckers more than trees do that are raised in any other way. Fruit trees raised from suckers do not bear so abundantly, and such good fruit, as trees raised from cuttings, slips or layers. A sucker is, in fact, a little tree with more or less of root to it, and is, of course, to be treated as a *tree*.

280.

BUDDING.

To have fruit trees by this method, or by that of *grafting*, you must first have *stocks*; that is to say, a young tree to bud or graft upon. What are the *sorts* of stocks proper for the sorts of fruit-trees respectively will be mentioned under the names of the latter. The stock is a *young tree* of some sort or other, and the *bud* is put into the bark on the side of this young tree during the summer; and not before the bud be full and plump. The work may generally be done all through the months of July and August, and, perhaps, later.

281.

GRAFTING.

Grafting is the joining of a cutting of one to another tree in such a way as that the tree, on which the cutting is placed, sends up its sap into the cutting, and makes it grow and become a tree. Now, as to the way, in which this, and the way in which *budding,* is *done,* they cannot upon any principle consistent with common sense, become matter of *written* description. Each is a mechanical operation, embracing numerous movements of the arms, hands, and fingers, and is no more to be taught by written directions than the making of a chest of drawers is. To *read* a full and minute account of the *acts* of budding and grafting would require ten times the space of time that it requires to go to a neighbour's and learn, from a *sight* of the operation, that which, after all, no written directions would ever teach. To bud and graft, in all the various modes, form a much nicer and more complicated operation than that of *making a shoe;* and I defy any human being to describe adequately all the several acts in the making of a shoe, in less than two volumes, each larger than this. The season for *taking off the cuttings* for grafts, is any time between Christmas and March. Any time after the sap is completely in a quiescent state and before it be again in motion. When cut off they will keep *several months.* I cut some *here* in January last (1819.) They reached England in *March;* and, I hear that they were growing well in June. A great deal has been said about the *season for grafting,* and Mr. MARSHALL tells the English, that it must not be done till the sap in the stock is *just ready to flow freely.* He has never seen an American Negro-man sitting by a hot six-plate stove, grafting apple-trees in the month of January, and then putting them away in his cave, to be brought out and planted in April! I have seen this; and my opinion is, that the work may be done at any time between

October and May: nay, I am not sure, that it may not be done all the summer long. The cuttings too, may be taken off, and put on directly; and, the sooner the better; but, in the winter months, they will keep good off the tree for several months.

282.

STOCKS.

Stocks must be of different ages and sizes in different cases; and even the propagation of the stocks themselves is not to be overlooked. Stocks are formed out of *suckers,* or raised from the *seed;* and the latter is by far the best; for suckers produce suckers, and do not grow to a handsome stem, or trunk. *Crabs* are generally the stocks for Apple-grafts, and *Plumbs* for Pears, Peaches, Nectarines, and Apricots. However, we shall speak of the *sorts of Stocks,* suitable to each sort of fruit-tree by and by: at present we have to speak of the *raising of Stocks.* If the stocks be to be of crabs or apples, the seeds of these should be collected in the fall when the fruit is ripe. They are generally got out by mashing the crabs, or apples. When the seeds are collected, put them immediately into fine earth; or sow them at once. It may not, however, be convenient to sow them at once; and, perhaps, the best way is to sow very early in the spring. If the stocks be to be of *stone* fruit, the stones, as of cherries, plumbs, peaches, and others, must be got when the fruit is ripe. The best way is to put them into fine earth, and keep them there till spring. The earth may be placed in a cellar; or put into a barrel; or, a little pit may be made in the ground, and it may be placed there. When the winter breaks up, dig a piece of ground *deep* and make it *rich;* make it very fine; form it into beds, three feet wide; draw drills across it at 8 inches distance; make them from two to three inches deep; put in the seeds pretty thick (for they cost little;) cover them completely; tread the earth down upon them; and then smooth the surface. When the plants come up, thin them to about 3 inches apart; and keep the ground between them perfectly clean during the summer. Hoe frequently; but *not deep near the plants;* for, we are speaking of *trees* here;

and trees do not renew their roots quickly as a cabbage, or a turnip, does. These young trees should be kept, during the first summer, as *moist* as possible, without watering; and the way to keep them as moist as possible is to keep the ground perfectly clean, and to hoe it frequently. I cannot help observing here upon an observation of Mr. MARSHALL: "as to *weeding*," says he, "though seedling trees must not be *smothered,* yet some *small weeds* may be suffered to grow in summer, as they help to *shade* the plants and keep the ground *cool.*" Mercy on this Gentleman's readers! Mr. Marshall had not read TULL; if he had, he never would have written this very erroneous sentence. It is the *root* of the weed that does the mischief. Let there be a rod of ground well set with even *"small weeds,"* and another rod *kept weeded.* Let them adjoin each other. Go, after 15 or 20 days of dry weather; examine the two; and you will find the weedless ground moist and fresh, while the other is dry as dust to a foot deep. The root of the weed sucks up every particle of moisture. What pretty things they are, then, to keep seedling trees *cool!*—To proceed: these seedlings, if well managed, will be eight inches high, and some higher, at the end of the first summer. The next spring they should be taken up; or, this may be done in the fall. They should be planted in rows, four feet apart, to give room to turn about amongst them; and at two feet apart in the rows, if intended to be grafted or budded without being again removed. If intended to be again removed, before grafting or budding, they may be put at a foot apart. They should be kept clean by hoeing between them, and the ground between them should be *dug in the fall,* but not at any other season of the year.—The plants will grow fast or slowly according to the soil and management; and, he who knows how to bud or to graft, will know when the stock is arrived at the proper size for each purpose.—To speak of the *kind* of stocks, most suitable to the different kinds of fruit trees, is reserved till we come to speak of the trees themselves; but there are some remarks to be made here, which have a *general application,* relative to the kinds of stocks.—It is supposed by some persons, that the nature of the stock affects the nature of the *fruit;* that is to say, that the fruit growing on branches, proceeding from a *bud,* or a *graft,* partakes, more or less of the flavour of *the fruit which would have grown on the stock,* if the stock had been suffered to grow to a tree and to bear fruit. This is Mr. MAR- SHALL'S notion. But, how erroneous it is must be manifest to every one when he reflects, that the stock for the *pear* tree is frequently the *white-thorn.* Can a pear partake of the nature of the *haw,* which grows upon the thorn, and which is a *stone-fruit* too? If this notion were correct, there could be hardly a single apple-orchard in all England: for, they graft upon *crab-stocks;* and, of course, all the apples, in the course of years, would become crabs. Apricots and Peaches are, in England, *always* put on plum-stocks; yet, after cen- turies of this practice, they do not become plumbs. If the *fruit* of the graft partake of the nature of the stock, why not the *wood* and *leaves?* Yet, is it not visible to all eyes, that neither ever does so partake?— This, then, like the carrying of the farina from the *male* to the *female* flower, is a mere whim, or dream. The bud, or graft, retains its own nature, wholly unchanged by the stock; and, all that is of conse- quence, as to the kind of stock, is, whether it be such as will *last long,* and supply the tree with *a suitable quantity of wood.* This is a matter of great importance; for, though *peach will grow on peach,* and *apple* on *apple,* the trees are not nearly so vigorous and durable as if the peach were put on the *plum* and the apple on the *crab.* In 1800, I sent several trees from England to Messrs. James and Thomas Paul, at Busleton, in Pennsylvania. There was a *Nectarine* amongst these. It is well known, that, in 1817, there had been so great a mortality in the peach orchards, that they had become almost wholly extinct. At Busleton there had been as great a mortality as in any other part. Yet I, that year, saw the *Nectarine tree* large, *sound in every part,* fine and *flourishing.* It is very well known, that the peach trees here are very *short-lived.* Six, seven, or eight years, seem to be the duration of their life. This *Nectarine* had stood *seventeen years,* and was likely to stand twice as long yet to come. It is now growing in the garden of the late Mr. James Paul, in Lower Dublin Township; and there any one may see it.—It is clear to me, therefore, that the short life of the peach-orchards is owing to the *stock being peach*. No small part of the peach-trees are raised *from the stone*. Nothing is more frequent than to see a farmer, or his wife, when he or she has eaten a good peach, go and make a little hole and *put the stone in the ground*, in order to have *a peach tree of the same sort*! Not considering, that the stone never, except by *mere accident*, produces fruit of the same quality as that within which it was contained, any more than the seed of a carnation produces flowers like those from which they proceeded.— The peaches in America are, when budded, put on *peach-stocks;* and this, I think, is the cause of their *swift decay*. They should be put on *plum-stocks;* for, to what other cause are we to ascribe the long life and vigorous state of the Nectarine at Mr. Paul's? The plum is a *closer* and *harder* wood than the peach. The peach-trees are destroyed by a *worm*, or, rather, a sort of *maggot*, that eats into *the bark at the stem*. The insects do not like the plum bark; and, besides, the plum is a more *hardy* and *vigorous* tree than the peach, and, observe, it is frequently, and most frequently, the feebleness, or sickliness, of the tree that *creates the insects*, and not the insects that create the feebleness and sickliness. There are thousands of peach trees in England and France that are *fifty years old*, and that are still in vigorous fruitfulness. There is a good deal in *climate*, to be sure; but, I am convinced, that there is a great deal in the *stock*.—Before I quit the subject of stocks, let me beg the reader never, if he can avoid it, to make use of *suckers*, particularly for an *apple or pear-orchard*, which almost necessarily is to become pasture. Stocks formed out of *suckers* produce *suckers;* and, if the ground remain in grass for a few years, there will arise a *young wood* all over the ground; and this wood, if not torn up by the plough, will, in a short time, *destroy the trees*, and will in still less time, deprive them of their fruitfulness. Besides this, suckers, being originally *excrescences*, and *unnaturally vigorous*, make wood *too fast*, make *too much wood;* and, where this is the case, the fruit is scanty in quantity. "Haste makes waste" in most cases; but, perhaps, in nothing so much as in the use of suckers as stocks. By waiting a year longer and bestowing a little care, you obtain seedling stocks; and, really, if a man has not the trifling portion of patience and industry that is here required, he is unworthy of the good fruit and the abundant crops, which with proper management, are sure, in this country, to be the reward of his pains.—Look at England, in the spring! There you see fruit trees of all sorts *covered with bloom;* and from all of it there sometimes comes, at last, not a single fruit. Here, is this favoured country, to count the blossoms is to count the fruit! The way to show our gratitude to God for such a blessing, is, to act well *our* part in turning the blessing to the best account.

PLANTING.
283.

I am not to speak here of the situation for planting, of the aspect, of the nature of the soil, of the preparation of the soil; for these have all been described in CHAPTER I, Paragraph 20, save and except, that, for trees, the ground should be prepared as directed for *Asparagus,* which see in its Alphabetical place, in Chapter IV.

284.

Before the reader proceed further, he should read very attentively what is said of *transplanting generally,* in Chapter III, Paragraph 109 and onwards. He will there perceive the absolute necessity of the ground, to be planted in, being made perfectly *fine,* and that no clods, great or small, ought to be tumbled in about the roots. This is so capital a point, that I must request the reader to pay particular attention to it. To remove a *tree,* though young, is an operation that puts the vegetative faculties to a severe test; and, therefore, every thing should be done to render the shock as little injurious as possible.

285.

The tree to be planted should be *as young* as circumstances will allow. The *season* is just when the *leaves become yellow,* or, as *early as possible in the spring.* The ground being prepared, and the tree taken up, prune the roots with a sharp knife so as to leave none more than about a foot long; and, if any have been torn off nearer to the stem, prune the part, so that no *bruises* or *ragged parts* remain. Cut off *all the fibres* close to the roots; for, they never live, and they *mould,* and do great injury. If cut off, their place is supplied by other fibres more quickly. Dig the hole to plant in three times as wide, and six inches deeper, than the roots actually need as mere room. And now, besides the fine earth generally, have some good mould *sifted.* Lay some of this six inches deep at the bottom of the hole. Place the roots upon this in their natural order, and hold the tree perfectly upright, while you put more sifted earth on the roots. Sway the tree backward and forward a little, and give it a gentle lift and shake, so that the fine earth may find its way amongst the roots and leave not the smallest cavity. Every root should be closely touched by the earth in every part. When you have covered all the roots with the sifted earth, and have seen that your tree stands just *as high* with regard to the level of the ground as it did in the place where it before stood, allowing about 3 inches for sinking, fill up the rest of the hole with the common earth of the plat, and when you have about half filled it, *tread* the earth that you put in, but not very hard. Put on the rest of the earth, and leave the surface perfectly smooth. Do not *water* by any means. Water, poured on, in this case, sinks rapidly down, and makes cavities amongst the roots. Lets in air. Mould and canker follow; and great injury is done.

286.

If the tree be planted in the fall, as soon as the leaf begins to be *yellow;* that is to say, in October early, it will have struck out new roots to the length of some inches before the winter sets in. And this is certainly the best time for doing the business. But, mind, the roots should be *out of ground* as short a time as possible; and should by no means be permitted to get *dry*, if you can avoid it; for, though some trees will *live* after having been a long while out of ground, the shorter the time out of ground the sooner the roots strike; and, if the roots should get dry before planting, they ought to be soaked in water, rain or pond, for half a day before the tree be planted.

287.

If the tree be for an orchard, it must be five or six feet high, unless cattle are to be kept out for two or three years. And, in this case, the head of the tree must be pruned short, to prevent it from swaying about from the force of the wind. Even when pruned, it will be exposed to be loosened by this cause, and must be kept steady by a stake; but, it must not be fastened to a stake, until rain has come to *settle the ground;* for, such fastening would prevent it from *sinking with the earth.* The earth would sink from it, and leave cavities about the roots.

288.

When the trees are *short,* they will require no stakes. They may be planted the second year after budding, and the first after grafting; and these are the best times. If planted in the fall, the tree should be shortened very early in the spring, and in such a way as to answer the ends to be pointed out more particularly when we come to speak of pruning.

289.

If you plant *in the spring,* it should be as early as the ground will bear moving; only, bear in mind, that the ground must always be *dry at top* when you plant. In this case, the new roots will strike out almost immediately; and as soon as the buds begin to *swell,* shorten the head of the tree. After a spring-planting, it may be necessary to guard against *drought;* and the best protection is the laying of small stones of any sort round the tree, so as to cover the area of a circle of three feet in diameter, of which circle the stem of the tree is the centre. This will keep the ground *cooler* than any thing else that you can put upon it.

290.

As to the *distances, at which trees ought* to be planted, that must depend on the sort of tree, and on other circumstances. It will be seen by looking at the plan of the garden (*Plate* 1,) that I make provision for 70 trees, and for a row of *grape vines* extending the length of two of the plats. The trees will have a space of 14 feet square each. But, in *orchards,* the distances for apples and pears must be much greater; otherwise the trees will soon run their branches into, and injure each other.

CULTIVATION.

291.

The Cultivation of fruit trees divides itself into two distinct parts; the management of the tree itself, which consists of *pruning* and *tying;* and the management of the ground where the trees grow, which consists of *digging, hoeing,* and *manuring.* The management of the tree itself differs with the sort of tree; and, therefore, I shall treat of the management of each sort under its own particular name. But the management of the *ground* where trees grow is the same in the case of all the larger trees; and, for that reason, I shall here give directions concerning it.

292.

In the first place, the ground is always to be kept *clear of weeds;* for, whatever they take is just so much taken from the fruit, either in quantity, or in quality, or in both. It is true, that very fine orchards have grass covering all the ground beneath the trees; but, these orchards would be still *finer* if the ground were kept clear from all plants whatever except the trees. Such a piece of ground is, at once, an Orchard and a Pasture: what is lost one way is, probably, gained the other. But, if we come to fine and choice fruits, there can be nothing that can grow beneath to balance against the injury done to the trees.

293.

The roots of trees *go deep;* but, the principal part of their *nourishment* comes from the top-soil. The ground should be loose to a good depth, which is the certain cause of constant moisture; but trees draw downwards as well as upwards, and draw more nourishment in the former than in the latter direction. *Vineyards,* as TULL observes, must always be *tilled,* in some way or other; or they will produce nothing of value. He adds, that Mr. EVELYN says, that "when the soil, wherein fruit-trees are planted, is constantly kept in tillage, they grow up to an Orchard in half the time, they would do, if the soil were not tilled." Therefore, tillage is useful; but, it were better, that there were tillage without under crops; for these crops take away a great part of the strength that the manure and tillage bring.

294.

Now, then, as to the trees in my *garden;* they are to be choice peaches, nectarines, apricots, plums, cherries, and grape vines, with a very few apples and pears. The *sorts* will be mentioned hereafter in the Alphabetical list; but, the tillage for all except the *grape vines,* is the same; and the nature of that exception will be particularly stated under the name of *grape.*

295.

It was observed before, that the ground is always to be kept *clear of weeds.* From the spring to the fall *frequent hoeing* all the ground over, not only to keep away weeds but to keep the ground moist in hot and dry weather, taking care never to hoe but when the ground is *dry at top.* This hoeing should not go deeper than four or five inches; for, there is a great difference between *trees* and *herbaceous plants* as to the *renewal of their roots* respectively. Cut off the lateral roots of a cabbage, or a turnip, of a wheat or a rye or an Indian-corn plant, and new roots, from the parts that remain, come out in 12 hours, and the operation, by multiplying the mouths of the feeders of the plant, gives it additional force. But, the roots of a tree consist of *wood,* more or less *hard;* they do not quickly renew themselves: they are of a permanent nature: and they must not be much mutilated during the time that the sap is in the flow.

296.

Therefore, the ploughing between trees or the digging between trees ought to take place only *in the fall,* which gives time for a renewal, or new supply, of roots before the sap be again in motion. For this reason, if crops be grown under trees in orchards, they should be of wheat, rye, winter-barley, or of something that does not demand a ploughing of the ground in the spring. In the garden, dig the ground well and clean, *with a fork,* late in November. Go close to the stems of the trees; but do not bruise the large roots. Clean and clear all well close round the stem. Make the ground smooth just there. Ascertain whether there be *insects* there of any sort. And, if there be, take care to destroy them. Pull, or scrape, off all rough bark at the bottom of the stem. If you even *peel off the outside bark* a foot or two up, in case there be insects, it will be the better. Wash the stems with water, in which *tobacco* has been soaked; and do this, whether you find insects or not. Put the tobacco into hot water, and let it soak 24 hours, before you use the water. This will destroy, or drive away, all insects.

297.

But, though, for the purpose of removing all harbour for insects, you make the ground smooth just round the stem of the tree, let the rest of the ground lay as rough as you can; for the rougher it lies the more will it be broken by the frost, which is a great enricher of all land. When the spring comes, and the ground is dry at the top, give the whole of the ground a good deep hoeing, which will make it level and smooth enough. Then go on again hoeing throughout the summer, and watching well all attempts of insects on the stems and bark of the trees.

298.

Diseases of trees are various in their kind; but, nine times out of ten they proceed from the *root*. Insects are much more frequently an *effect* than a *cause*. If the disease proceed from *blight*, there is no prevention, except that which is suggested by the fact, that feeble and sickly trees are frequently blighted when healthy ones are not; but, when the insects come, they add greatly to the evil. They are generally produced by the disease, as maggots are by putrefaction. The *ants* are the only active insect for which there is not a cure; and I know of no means of destroying them, but finding out their nests, and pouring boiling water on them. A line dipped in *tar* tied round the stem, will keep them from climbing the tree: but they are still alive. As to the diminutive creatures that appear as *specks in the bark;* the best, and perhaps, the only remedy against the species of disease of which they are the symptoms, consists of good plants, good planting and good tillage. When orchards are seized with diseases that pervade the whole of the trees, or nearly the whole, the best way is to cut them down: they are more plague than profit, and, as long as they exist, they are a source of nothing but constantly-returning disappointment and mortification. However, as there are persons who have a delight in quackery, who are never so happy as when they have some specific to apply, and to whom rosy cheeks and ruby lips are almost an eye-sore, it is, perhaps, fortunate, that the vegetable world presents them with patients; and thus, even in the cotton-blight or canker, we see an evil, which we may be led to hope is not altogether unaccompanied with good.

LIST OF FRUITS.
299.

Having, in the former parts of this CHAPTER, treated of the propagation, planting, and cultivation of *all fruit trees* (the grape vine only excepted) it would remain for me merely to give a List of the several fruits; to speak of the different sorts of each; and of the mode of preserving them; but the *stocks* and *pruning* vary, in some cases; and, therefore, as I go along, I shall have to speak of them. Before, however, I enter on this Alphabetical List, let me observe, that only a part of the fruits mentioned in it are proposed to be raised in the *garden;* and that the 70 trees, shown in the *Plate* I, are intended to mark the paces, and, in some degree, the form, of 6 Apple trees, 6 Apricots, 6 Cherries, 6 Nectarines, 30 Peaches, 6 Pears, and 10 Plums; and, that the trelises, on the Southern sides of Plats, No. 8 and 9, are intended to mark the places for 4 Grape-Vines, there being another *Plate* to explain more fully the object and dimensions of this trelis work.

300.
APPLE.

Apples are usually grafted on *crab-stocks* (See Paragraph 282;) but, when you do not want the trees to grow tall and large, it is better to raise stocks from the seed of some Apple not much given to produce large wood. Perhaps the Fall-Pippin seed may be as good as any. When you have planted the tree, as directed in Paragraphs 283 to 289, and when the time comes for shortening the head, cut it off so as to leave only five or six joints or buds. These will send out *shoots,* which will become *limbs.* The tree will be what they call, in England, a *dwarf standard;* and, of this description are to be all the 70 trees in the garden.—As to *pruning,* see PEACH; for, the pruning of all these dwarf standards is nearly the same.—The sorts of Apples are numerous, and every body knows, pretty well, which are the best. In my garden I should only have six apple trees; and, therefore, they should be of the finest for the season at which they are eaten. The earliest apple is the *Junating,* the next the *Summer Pearmain.* Besides these I would have a *Doctor-apple,* a *Fall-Pippin,* a *Newtown Pippin* and a *Greening.* The quantity would not be very large that six trees would produce; yet it would be considerable, and the quality would be exquisitely fine. I would not suffer too great a number of fruit to remain on the tree; and, I would be bound to have the three last-named sorts weighing, on an average, 12 ounces. I have seen a Fall-Pippin that weighed *a pound.*—To *preserve* apples, in their whole state, observe this, that *frost* does not much injure them, provided they be kept in *total darkness* during the frost and until they be used, and provided they be perfectly *dry* when put away. If put together in large parcels, and kept from the frost, they *heat,* and then they *rot;* and, those of them that happen not to rot, lose their flavour, become vapid, and are, indeed, good for little. This is the case with the Newtown Pippins that are *sent to England,* which are half lost by *rot,* while the remainder are poor tasteless stuff, very little better than the English apples, the far greater part of which are either sour or mawkish. The apples thus sent, have every possible disadvantage. They are *gathered carelessly;* tossed into baskets and tumbled into barrels at once, and without any packing stuff between them; the barrels are flung into and out of wagons; they are rolled along upon pavements; they are put in the hold, or between the decks, of the ship: and, is it any wonder, that a barrel of *pomace,* instead of *apples,* arrive at Liverpool or London? If, instead of this careless work, the apples were gathered (*a week before ripe;*) not bruised at all in the gathering; laid in the sun, on boards or cloths, three days, to let the watery particles evaporate a little; put into barrels with fine-cut straw-chaff, in such a way as that no apple touched another; carefully carried to the ship and put on board, and as carefully landed; and if this were the mode, one barrel, though it would contain only *half the quantity,* would sell for as much as, upon an average, taking in loss by total destruction, twenty barrels sell for now. *On* the deck is the best part of the ship for apples; but, if managed as I have directed, *between decks* would do very well.—In the keeping of apples for market, or for home-use, the same precautions ought to be observed as to *gathering* and *laying out to dry;* and, perhaps, to pack in the same way also is the best mode that can be discovered. *Dried Apples* is an article of great and general use. Every body knows, that the apples are peeled, cut into about eight pieces, the core taken out, and the pieces put in the sun till they become dry and tough. They are then put by in bags, or boxes, in a dry place. But, the flesh of the apple does not change its *nature* in the drying; and, therefore, the *finest,* and not the *coarsest,* apples should have all this trouble bestowed upon them.

301.
APRICOT.

This is a very delightful fruit. It comes earlier than the peach: and some like it better. It is a hardier tree, bears as well as the peach, and the green fruit, when the size of a hickory-nut, makes a very good tart. When ripe, or nearly ripe, it makes a better pie than the peach; and the tree, when well raised, planted, and cultivated, will *last a century.*—Apricots are budded or grafted upon *plum stocks,* or upon stocks raised from Apricot-stones. They do not bear so soon as the peach by one year. For the pruning of them, see PEACH.—— There are many sorts of *Apricots;* some come earlier, some are larger, and some finer than others. It may be sufficient to name the *Brussels,* the *Moore-Park,* and the *Turkey.* The first carries most fruit as to number; but, the others are larger and of finer flavour. Perhaps two trees of each of these sorts would be the most judicious selec- tion. I have heard, that the *Apricot* does not *do* in this country! That is to say, I suppose, it will not *do of its own accord,* like a peach, by having the *stone flung upon the ground,* which it certainly will not; and it is very much to be commended for refusing to *do* in this way. But, properly managed, I know it will *do,* for I never tasted finer Apricots than I have in America; and, indeed, who can believe that it will not *do* in a country, where there are no blights of fruit trees worth speaking of, and where melons ripen to such perfection in the natural ground and almost without care?

302.

BARBERRY.

This fruit is well known. The tree, or shrub, on which it grows, is raised from the *seed,* or from *suckers,* or layers. Its place ought to be in the *South Border;* for, the hot sun is rather against its fruit growing large.

303.

CHERRY.

Cherries are budded or grafted upon stocks raised from cherry-stones of any sort. If you want the tree tall and large, the stock should come from the small black cherry tree that grows wild in the woods. If you want it *dwarf,* sow the stones of a *morello* or a *May-duke.* The sorts of cherries are very numerous; but, the six trees for my garden should be, a *May-cherry,* a *May-duke,* a *black-heart,* a *white-heart,* and *two bigeroons.* The four former are well known in America, but I never saw but two trees of the last, and those I sent from England to Bustleton, in Pennsylvania, in the year 1800. They are now growing there, in the gardens of the two Messrs. Paul's. Cuttings from them have been carried and used as grafts all round the country. During the few days that I was at Mr. James Paul's, in 1817, several persons came for grafts; so that these trees must be pretty famous. The fruit is large, thin skinned, small stone, and fine colour and flavour, and the tree grows freely and in beautiful form.—For *Pruning,* see PEACH.—To *preserve* cherries, gather them *without bruising;* take off the tails; lay them in the sun on dry deal boards; when quite dry put them by in bags in a dry place. They form a variety in the tart-making way.

304.

CHESTNUT.

This is an inhabitant of the woods; and, as to its *fruit*, I have only to say, that the American is as much better than the Spanish as the tree is a finer tree.—To *preserve* chestnuts, so as to have them to sow in the spring, or to eat through the winter, you must put them into a box, or barrel, mixed with, and covered over by, *fine dry sand*. If there be *maggots* in any of the chestnuts, they will work up through the sand, to get to air; and, thus, you have your chestnuts sweet and sound and fresh. To know whether chestnuts will *grow*, toss them into water. If they *swim*, they will not grow.

305.

CRANBERRY.

This is one of the best fruits in the world. All tarts sink out of sight in point of merit, when compared with that made of the American Cranberry. There is a little dark red thing, about as big as a large pea, sent to England from the North of Europe, and is *called* a Cranberry; but, it does not resemble the American in taste any more than in bulk.—It is well known that this valuable fruit is, in many parts of this country, spread over the low lands in great profusion; and that the mere gathering of it is all that bountiful nature requires at our hands.—This fruit is preserved all the year, by stewing and putting into jars, and when taken thence is better than currant jelly. The fruit, in its whole state, laid in a heap, in a dry room, will keep sound and perfectly good for six months. It will freeze and thaw and freeze and thaw again without receiving any injury. It may, if you choose, be kept in water all the while, without any injury. I received a barrel in England, mixed with water, as good and as fresh as I ever tasted at New York or Philadelphia.

306.

CURRANT.

There are *red, white* and *black,* all well known. Some persons like one best, and some another. The propagation and cultivation of all the sorts are the same. The currant tree is propagated from *cuttings;* and the cuttings are treated as has been seen in Paragraph 276. When the tree has stood two years in the Nursery, plant it where it is to stand; and take care that it has only *one stem.* Let no limbs come out to grow nearer than six inches of the ground. Prune the tree every year. Keep it *thin of wood.* Keep the middle open and the limbs extended; and when these get to about three feet in length, cut off, every winter, *all the last year's shoots.* If you do not attend to this, the tree will be nothing but a great bunch of twigs, and you will have very little fruit. Cultivate and manure the ground as for other fruit trees. See Paragraphs 289 to 296. In this country the currant requires *shade* in summer. If exposed to the full sun, the fruit is apt to become too sour. Plant it, therefore, in the South Border.

307.

FIG.

There are several sorts of Figs, but all would *ripen* in this country. The only difficulty must be to protect the trees *in winter,* which can hardly be done without covering pretty closely. Figs are raised either from *cuttings* or *layers,* which are treated as other cuttings and layers are. See Paragraphs 276 and 278. The fig is a *mawkish* thing at best; and, amongst such quantities of fine fruit as this country produces, it can, from mere curiosity only, be thought worth raising at all, and especially at great trouble.

308.

FILBERD.

This is a sort of *Nut,* oblong in shape, very thin in the shell, and in flavour as much superior to the common nut as a Water-melon is to a pumpkin. The American nut tree is a *dwarf* shrub. The Filberd is a tall one, and will, under favourable circumstances, reach the height of *thirty feet*. I never saw any Filberd trees in this country, except those that I sent from England in 1800. They are six in number, and they are now growing in the garden of the late Mr. JAMES PAUL, of Lower Dublin Township, in Philadelphia county. I saw them in 1817, when they were, I should suppose, about 20 feet high. They had always borne, I was told, very large quantities, never failing. Perhaps five or six bushels a year, measured in the husk, a produce very seldom witnessed in England; so that, there is no doubt that the climate is extremely favourable to them. Indeed to what, that is good for man, is it not favourable?—The Filberd is propagated from *layers*, or from *suckers*, of which latter it sends forth great abundance. The layers are treated like other layers, (See Paragraph 278,) and they very soon become trees. The suckers are also treated like other suckers. (See Paragraph 279;) but, layers are preferable, for the reasons before stated.—This tree cannot be propagated from *seed* to bear *Filberds*. The seed, if sown, will produce *trees;* but, those trees will bear poor thick-shelled nuts, except it be by mere accident. It is useful to know how to *preserve* the fruit; for it is very pleasant to have it all the winter long. Always let the filberds hang on the tree till *quite ripe*, and that is ascertained by their coming out of the husk without any effort. They are then *brown*, and the butt ends of them *white*. Lay them in the sun for a day to dry; then put them in a box, or jar, or barrel, with very fine *dry sand*. Four times as much sand as filberds, and put them in any dry place. Here they will keep well till April or May; and, perhaps, longer. This is better a great deal than putting them, as they do in England, into jars, and the jars into a cellar; for if they do not *mould* in that situation, they lose much of their sweetness in a few months. The burning sun is apt to scorch up the leaves of the Filberd tree. I would, therefore, plant a row of them as near as possible to the South fence. Ten trees at eight feet apart might be enough—The Filberd will do very well *under the shade of lofty trees*, if those trees do not stand too thick. And it is by no means an ugly shrub, while the wood of it is, as well as the nut wood, which is, in England, called *hazel,* and is a very good wood. In the oak-woods there, hazel is very frequently the *underwood;* and it makes small hoops, and is applied to various other purposes.—I cannot dismiss this article without exhorting the American farmer to provide himself with some of this sort of tree, which, when small, is easily conveyed to any distance in winter, and got ready to plant out in the spring. Those that are growing at Mr. PAUL's were dug up, in England, in January, shipped to New York, carried on the top of the stage, in the dead of winter to Busleton, kept in a cellar till spring, and then planted out. These were the first trees of the kind, as far as I have been able to learn, that ever found their way to this country. I hear that Mr. STEPHEN GIRARD takes to himself the act of first introduction, from France. But, I must deny him this. He, I am told, brought his trees several years later than I sent mine.

309.

GOOSEBERRY.

Various are the sorts, and no one that is not good. The shrub is propagated precisely like that of the currant. I cannot tell the cause that it is so little cultivated in America. I should think (though I am by no means sure of the fact) that it would do very well under the shade of a South Fence. However, as far as the fruit is useful in its *green* state, for tarts, the *Rhubarb* supplies its place very well. The fruit is excellent when well raised. They have gooseberries in England nearly as large as pigeon's eggs, and the crops that the trees bear are prodigious.

310.

GRAPE.

This is a very important article; and, before I proceed to treat of the culture of the grape-vine, I must notice the astonishing circumstance, that that culture should be almost wholly unknown in this country of *fine sun.* I have asked the *reason* of this, seeing that the fruit is so good, the crop so certain, and culture so easy. The only answer that I have received is, that the *rose-bug* destroys the fruit. Now, this I know, that I had a grape vine in my court-yard at Philadelphia; that it bore nothing the first year; that I made an arched trelis for it to run over; and that I had hundreds of pounds of fine grapes hanging down in large bunches. Yes, I am told, but this was in a city; and amongst *houses,* and *there* the grapes do very well. Then, 1799, I saw, at Spring Mills, on the banks of the Schuylkill, in Pennsylvania, the Vineyard of Mr. *Le Gau,* which covered about two acres of ground, and the vines of which were loaded with fine grapes of, at least, twenty different sorts. The vineyard was on the side of a little hill; on the top of the hill was a cornfield, and in the front of it, across a little valley, and on the side of another little hill, was a wood of lofty trees; the country in general, being very much covered with woods. Mr. LE GAU made wine from this Vineyard. The vines are planted at about four feet apart, grew upright, and were tied to sticks about five feet high, after the manner of some, at least, of the vineyards of France.—Now, are not these facts alone decisive in the negative of the proposition, that there is a generally prevalent obstacle to the growing of grapes in this country?—Mr. HULME, in his Journal to the West (See my Year's Residence, Paragraph 892,) gives an account of the *Vineyards* and of the *wine* made, at VEVAY, on the OHIO. He says, that, that year, about *five thousand gallons* of wine were made; and, he observes, what more can be wanted for the grape-vine, than *rich land* and *hot sun.*—Besides, is not the grape-vine a *native* here? There are many different sorts of grapes, that grow in the woods, climb the trees, cover some of them over, and bear and ripen their fruit. How often do we meet with a vine, in the autumn, with Grapes, called chicken grapes, hanging on it from every bough of an oak or some other timber-tree! This grape resembles, as nearly as possible, what is, in England, called the *Black cluster;* and, unquestionably, only wants cultivation to give it as good a flavour. Does the *Rose bug* prevent these vines from bearing, or from ripening their fruit?—Taking it for granted, then, that this obstacle is *imaginary,* rather than real, I shall now proceed to speak of the propagation and cultivation of the grape-vine in the open ground of a garden, and, in doing this, I shall have frequently to refer to PLATE III.—The grape-vine is raised from *cuttings,* or from *layers.* As to the first, you cut off, *as early as the ground* is open in the spring, a piece of the *last year's wood;* that is to say, a piece of a shoot, which grew during the last summer. This cutting should, if convenient, have an inch or two of the former year's wood at the bottom of it; but, this is by no means absolutely necessary. The cutting should have *four or five buds or joints.* Make the ground rich, move it deep, and make it fine. Then put in the cutting with a setting-stick, leaving only two buds, or joints, above ground; fasten the cutting well in the ground; and, then, as to keeping it *cool* and moist, see *cuttings,* in Paragraph 276.—*Layers* from grave-vines are obtained with great ease. You have only to lay a shoot, or limb, however young or old, upon the ground, and cover any part of it with earth, it will strike out roots the first summer, and will become a vine, to be carried and planted in any other place. But, observe, vines do not *transplant well.* For this reason, both cuttings and layers, if intended to be removed, are usually *set,* or *layed,* in *flower-pots,* out of which they are turned, with the ball of earth along with them, into the earth where they are intended to grow and produce their fruit.—I have now to speak more particularly of the vines of my garden. PLATE I. represents, or, at least, I mean it to represent, on the south side of the *Plats* No. 8 and No. 9, two trelis works for vines. These are to be *five feet high,* and are to consist of two rows of little upright bars two inches and a half by two inches, put two feet into the ground, and made of *Locust,* and then they will, as you well know, last *for ever,* without paint and without any kind of trouble.—Now, then, bear in mind, that each of these Plats, is, from East to West, 70 feet long. Each will, there-

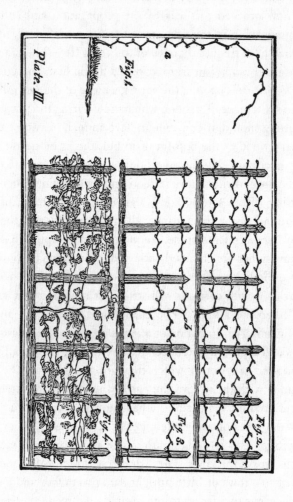

Plate. III

Fig. 1.

a

Fig. 4.

Fig. 3.

Fig. 2.

fore, take four vines, allowing to each vine an extent of 16 feet, and something more for overrunning branches.—Look, now, at PLATE III, which exhibits, in *all its dimensions,* the *cutting become a plant,* FIG. 1. The first year of its being a vine *after the leaves are off and before pruning,* FIG. 2. The same year's vine *pruned in winter,* FIG. 3. The vine, in the next summer, with shoots, leaves, and grapes, FIG. 4.—Having measured your distances, put in a cutting at each place where there is to be a vine. You are to leave two joints or buds out of ground. From these will come *two shoots* perhaps; and, if two come, rub off the top one and leave the bottom one, and, in winter, cut off the bit of dead wood which will, in this case, stand above the bottom shoot. Choose, however, the upper one to remain, if the lower one be very weak. Or, a better way is, to put in two or three cuttings within an inch or two of each other, leaving only *one bud* to each out of ground, and taking away, in the fall, the cuttings that send up the weakest shoots. The object is to get one good shoot coming out as near to the ground as possible.—This shoot you tie to an upright stick, letting it grow its full length. When winter comes, cut this shoot down to the bud nearest to the ground.—The next year another, and a much stronger shoot will come out; and, when the leaves are off, in the fall, this shoot will be eight or ten feet long, having been tied to a stake as it rose, and will present what is described in FIG. 1, PLATE III. You must make your trelis; that is, put in your upright *Locust-bars* to tie the next summer's shoots to. You will want (See FIG. 2.) eight shoots to come out to run horizontally, to be tied to these bars. You must now, then, in winter, cut off your vine, leaving *eight* buds, or joints. You see there is a mark for this cut, at *a,* fig. 1. During summer 8 shoots will come, and, as they proceed on, they must be tied with matting, or something soft, to the bars. The whole vine, both ways included, is supposed to go 16 feet; but, if your tillage be good, it will go much further, and then the ends must be cut off in winter.—Now, then, winter presents you your vine as in *fig.* 2; and now you must *prune,* which is the all-important part of the business.—Observe, and bear in mind, that little or no fruit ever comes on a grape-vine, except on young shoots that come out of wood of the *last year*. All the four last year's shoots that you find in *fig*. 2, would send out bearers; but, if you suffer that, you will have a great parcel of *small wood*, and little or no fruit next year. Therefore, cut off 4 of the last year's shoots, as at *b*. (*Fig*. 3.) leaving only *one bud*. The four other shoots will send out a shoot from every one of their buds, and, if the vine be *strong*, there will be *two bunches of grapes* on each of these young shoots; and, as the last year's shoots are supposed to be each 8 feet long, and as there generally is a bud at, or about, every half foot, every last year's shoot will produce 32 bunches of grapes; every vine 128 bunches; and the 8 vines 512; and, possibly, nay, probably, so many *pounds* of grapes! Is this incredible? Take, then, this well known fact, that there is a grape vine, a single vine, with only *one stem*, in the King of England's Gardens at his palace of Hampton Court, which has, for, perhaps, *half a century*, produced on an average, annually, *a ton of grapes*; that is to say, 2,240 pounds Avoirdupois weight. That vine covers a space of about 40 feet in length and 20 in breadth. And your two trelises, being, together, 128 feet long, and 4 deep, would form a space of more than half the dimensions of the vine of Hampton Court. However, suppose you have only a *fifth part* of what you might have, a hundred bunches of grapes are worth a great deal more than the annual trouble, which is, indeed, very little. *Fig*. 4 shows a vine in summer. You see the four shoots *bearing*, and four other shoots coming on for the next year, from the butts left at the winter pruning, as at *b*. These four latter you are to tie to the bars as they advance on during the summer.—When winter comes again, you are *to cut off the four shoots that sent out the bearers during the summer*, and leave the four that grew out of the butts. Cut the four old shoots that have borne, so as to *leave but one bud at the butt*. And they will then be sending out wood, while the other four will be sending out fruit. And thus you go on year after year for your life; for, as to the vine, it will, if well treated, outlive you and your children to the third and even thirtieth generation. I think they say, that the vine at Hampton Court was planted in the reign of King William.—During the summer there are two things to be observed, as to pruning. Each of the *last year's shoots* has 32 buds, and, of course, it sends out 32 shoots with the grapes on them, for the grapes come out of the 2 first fair buds of these shoots. So that here would be an enormous quantity of wood, if it were all left till the end of summer. But, this must not be. When the grapes get as big as *peas,* cut off the green shoots that bear them, at *two buds distance* from the fruit. This is necessary in order to clear the vine of confusion of branches, and also to keep the sap back for the supply of the fruit. These new shoots, that have the bunches on, must be kept tied to the trelis, or else the wind would tear them off. The other thing is, to take care to keep nicely tied to the bars the shoots that are to send forth bearers the next year; and, if you observe any little *side-shoots* coming out of them to crop these off as soon as they appear, leaving nothing but the clear, clean shoot. It may be remarked, that the butt, as at *b,* when it is cut off the next time, will be *longer by a bud.* That will be so; but, by the third year the vine will be so strong, that you may safely cut the shoots back to within six inches of the main trunk, leaving the new shoots to come out of it where they will; taking care to let but *one* grow for the summer. If shoots start out of the main trunk irregularly, rub them off as soon as they appear, and never suffer your vine to have any more than its regular number of shoots. As to *cultivation of the ground,* the ground should not only be deeply dug in the fall, but, with a fork, two or three times during the summer. They plough between them in Langue-doc, as we do between the Indian Corn. The ground should be manured every fall, with good rich manure. Blood of any kind is excellent for vines. But, in a word, the tillage and the manuring cannot be too good. All that now remains is to speak of the *sorts of grapes.* The climate of this country will ripen any sort of grape. But, it may be as well to have some that come *early*. The *Black July* grape, as it is called in England, or, as it is called in France, the *Noir Hatif,* is the earliest of all. I would have this for one of my eight vines; and, for the other seven I would have, the *Chasselas;* the *Burgundy;* the *Black Muscadine;* the *Black Frontinac;* the *Red Frontinac;* the *White Sweet Water;* and the *Black Hamburgh,* which is the sort of the Hampton-Court Vine.—In cases where grapes are to be grown against houses, or to be trained over bowers, the *principle* is the same, though the *form* may differ. If against the side of a house, the main stem of the vine might, by degrees, be made to go, I dare say, a *hundred feet high.* Suppose 40 feet. In that case, it would be *forty* instead of *four;* but the *side shoots,* or alternate bearing limbs, would still come out in the same manner. The stem, or side limbs, may, with the greatest ease, be made to accommodate themselves to windows, or to any interruptions of smoothness on the surface. If the side of the house, or place, be not very high, not more than 15 or 20 feet; the best way is to plant the vine in the middle of your space, and, instead of training an *upright* stem, take the two lowest shoots and lead them along, one from each side of the plant, to become stems, to lie along within six inches or a foot of the ground. These will, of course, send out shoots, which you will train *upright* against the building, and which you will cut out alternately, as directed in the other case.

311.

HUCKLEBERRY.

It is well known that it grows wild in great abundance, in many parts, and especially in Long Island, where it gives rise to a *holiday,* called *Huckleberry Monday.* It is a very good fruit for tarts mixed with Currants; and by no means bad to eat in its raw state.

312.

MADEIRA NUT.

See *Walnut.*

313.

MEDLAR.

A very poor thing indeed. The Medlar is propagated by grafting on *crab*-stocks, or pear-stocks. It is, at any rate, especially in this country, a thing not worthy of a place in a garden. At best, it is only one degree better than a *rotten apple*.

314.

MELON.

See *Melon* in Chapter IV.

315.

MULBERRY.

This tree is raised from *cuttings* or from *layers*. See Paragraphs 276 and 278. The *White-Mulberry*, which is the finest, and which the Silk worm feeds on, grows wild, and bears well, at two miles from the spot where I am now writing.

316.

NECTARINE.

As to propagation, planting and cultivation, the Nectarine is, in all respects, the same as the *peach*, which, therefore, see. It is certainly a *finer fruit*, especially the *Violet* Nectarine; but, it is not grown, or, but very little, in America. I cannot believe, that there is any insurmountable obstacle in the way. It is grown *in England* very well. The *White French* would certainly do here; and it is the most beautiful of fruit, and a greater bearer, though not so fine in flavour, as the *Violet*. The *Newington*, the *Roman*, are by no means so good. I would have in the *Garden* three trees of each of the two former.

317.

NUT.

Grows wild. Not worthy of a place in the Garden. Is propagated, and the fruit preserved, like *Filberd*, which see.

318.

PEACH.

The peach being the principal tree for the garden, I shall, under this head, give directions for *pruning* and *forming the tree.*—Peaches are propagated by *budding.* The *stock* should be of *plum,* for the reasons given in Paragraph 282.—The tree is to be *planted,* agreeably to the directions in Paragraphs 283 to 290. And now for the pruning and forming the tree. Look at PLATE IV. *fig.* 2, and *fig.* 3. The first is a peach tree such as I would have it at four or five years, old; the last is a peach tree such as we generally see at that age. The practice is to plant the tree, and to let it grow in its own way. The consequence is, that, in a few years, it runs up to a long naked stem with two or three long naked limbs, having some little weak boughs at the tops, and, the tree being top-heavy, is, nineteen times out of twenty, leaning on one side; and, it presents, altogether, a figure by no means handsome in itself or creditable to the owner.—This is *fig.* 3.—Now, to have *fig.* 2, the following is the way.—The tree should, in the first place, be budded very near to the ground. After it be planted, cut it down to within a foot and a half of the ground, and always cut sloping close to a bud. In this foot and a half, there will be many buds, and they will, the first summer, send out many shoots. Now, when shoots begin to appear, rub them all off but *three,* leave the top one, and one *on each side,* at suitable distances lower down. These will, in time become limbs. The next year, top the *upright* shoot (that came out of the top bud) again, so as to bring out other *horizontal limbs,* pointing in a different direction from those that came out the last year. Thus the tree will get a *spread.* After this, you must keep down the aspiring shoots; and, every winter, cut out some of the weak wood, that the tree may not be over-burdened with wood. If, in time, the tree be getting thin of bearing wood towards the trunk, cut some of the limbs back, and they will then send out many shoots, and fill up the naked places. The lowest limb of the tree, should come out of the trunk at not more than 9 or

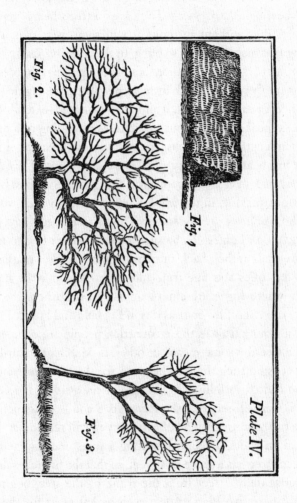

Fig. 1.

Fig. 2.

Fig. 3.

Plate IV.

10 inches from the ground. The greater part of the tree will be within the reach of a man from the ground; and a short step-ladder reaches the rest.—By this management the tree is always in a state of full bearing. *Always young.* To talk of a tree's being *worn out* is nonsense. But, without pruning, it will soon wear out. It is the pruning that makes it always young. In the *"Ecole du Jardin Potagur,"* by Monsieur DE COMBLES, there is an account of peach trees in full bearing at *fifty years old.* And, little do people here imagine to what a distance a peach tree will, if properly managed, extend. Mr. DE COMBLES speaks of numerous peach trees extending to more than *fifty feet* in length on the trelis, and *twelve feet* in breadth, or height, and in full bearing in every part. Here is a space of *six hundred square feet,* and, in case of a good crop, four peaches at least in every square foot, making, in the whole, 2,400 peaches, which would fill little short of *ten or twelve bushels.* This is to be seen any year at MONTREUIL in France. To be sure, these trees are tied to trelises, and have walls at their back; but, this climate requires neither; and, surely, fine trees and fine fruit and large crops may be had in a country where *blights* are almost unknown, and where the young fruit is *never* cut off by *frosts,* as it is in England and France. To preserve the young fruit in those countries, people are compelled to *cover* the trees by some means or other, in March and April. Here there needs no such thing. When you see the blossom, you know that the fruit is to follow. By looking at the *Plan* of the Garden, PLATE I, you will see, that the *Plats,* No. 8 and 9, contain 30 trees and the two vine-trelises. The *Plats* are, you will remember, 70 feet long and 56 wide. Of course, putting 5 trees one way and 4 the other, each tree has a space of 14 feet, so that the branches may extend horizontally 7 feet from the trunk of the tree, before they meet. In these two Plats 14 feet wide is left clear for the grape vines.—These 30 Peach-trees, properly managed, would yield more fruit, even *in bulk,* than a large orchard in the common way; and ten times as much in point of value; the size as well as the flavour of the

fruit are greatly improved by this mode of culture.—However, the *sort* is of very great consequence. It is curious enough, that people in general think little of the *sort* in the case of *peaches*, though they are so choice in the case of *apples*. A peach is *a peach*, it seems, though I know of no apples between which there is more difference than there is between different sorts of peaches, some of which melt in the mouth, while others are little better than a white turnip.—The sort is, then, a matter of the first importance; and, though the sorts are very numerous, the thirty trees that I would have should be as follows:—1 *Violette Hative*, 6 *Early Montaubon*, 1 *Vanguard*, 6 *Royul George*, 6 *Grosse Mignonne*, 4 *Early Noblesse*, 3 *Gallande*, 2 *Bellgarde*, 2 *Late Noblesse*. These are all to be had of Mr. PRINCE, of Flushing, in this island, and, as to his *word*, every body knows that it may be safely relied on. What is the trifling expense of 30 trees! And, when you once have them, you propagate from them for your life. Even for the feeding of hogs, a gallon of peaches of either of the above sorts is worth twenty gallons of the poor, pale, tasteless things that we see brought to market.—As to *dried* peaches, every body knows that they are managed as dried apples are; only that they must be gathered for this purpose before they be soft.

319.

PEAR.

Pears are grafted on *pear-stocks* or *quince-stocks*, or on those of the *white-thorn*. The last is best, because most *durable*; and, for dwarf trees, much the best, because they do not throw up wood so big and so lofty. For orchards, pear-stocks are best; but not from *suckers* on any account. They are sure to fill the orchard with suckers.—The *pruning* for your pear trees in the garden should be that of the *peach*. The pears will grow higher; but they may be made to spread at bottom, and that will keep them from towering too much. They should stand together, in one of the *Plats*, 10 or 11.—The sorts of pears are numerous; the six that I should choose are, the *Vergalouse*, the

Winter Bergamot, the *D'Auche,* the *Beurré,* the *Chaumontelle,* the *Winter Bonchretian.*

320.

PLUMS.

How is it that we see so few plums in America, when the markets are supplied with cart-loads in such a chilly, shady, and blighty country as England. A Green-gage Plum is very little inferior to the very finest peach; and I never tasted a better Green-gage than I have at New York. It must, therefore, be negligence. But Plums are prodigious *bearers,* too; and would be very good for hogs as well as peaches.—This tree is grafted upon plum-stocks, raised from *stones* by all means; for *suckers* send out a forest of suckers.—The pruning is precisely that of the peach.—The six trees that I would have in the garden should be 4 *Green-gages,* 1 *Orlean,* 1 *Blue Perdigron.*

321.

QUINCE.

Should grow in a moist place and in very rich ground. It is raised from *cuttings,* or *layers,* and these are treated like other cuttings and layers.—Quinces are dried like apples.

322.

RASPBERRY.

A sort of *woody herb,* but produces fruit that vies, in point of crop as well as flavour, with that of the proudest tree. I have never seen them fine in America since I saw them covering hundreds of thousands of acres of ground in the *Province of New Brunswick.* They come there even in the interstices of the *rocks,* and, when the August sun has parched up the leaves, the landscape is *red with the fruit.* Where woods have been burnt down, the raspberry and the huckleberry instantly spring up, divide the surface between them, and furnish autumnal food for flocks of pigeons that darken the earth beneath their flight. *Whence* these plants *come,* and cover spots thirty or forty miles square, which have been covered with woods for ages upon ages, I leave for philosophers to say, contenting myself with relating how they come and how they are treated in gardens.— They are raised from *suckers,* though they may be raised from *cuttings.* The suckers *of this year,* are planted out in rows, six feet apart, and the plants two feet apart in the rows. This is done in the fall, or early in the spring. At the time of planting they should be cut down to within *a foot* of the ground. They will bear a little, and they will send out several suckers which will bear the next year.—About four is enough to leave, and those of the strongest. These should be cut off in the fall, or early in spring, to within four feet of the ground, and should be tied to a small stake. A straight branch of *Locust* is best, and then the stake lasts a life-time at least, let the life be as long as it may. The next year more suckers come up, which are treated in the same way.—Fifty clumps are enough, if well managed.—There are *white* and *red,* some like one best and some the other. To have them fine, you must dig in manure in the Autumn, and keep the ground clean during the Summer by hoeing.— I have tried to *dry* the fruit; but it lost its flavour. *Raspberry-Jam* is a deep-red *sugar;* and raspberry-wine is red brandy, rum, or whiskey; neither having the taste of the fruit. To *eat* cherries, *preserved* in spirits, is only an apology, and a very poor and mean one, for dram-drinking; a practice which every man ought to avoid, and the very thought of giving way to which ought to make the cheek of a woman redden with shame.

323.

STRAWBERRY.

This plant is a native of the fields and woods here, as it is in Europe. There are many sorts, and all are improved by cultivation. The *Scarlet,* the *Alpine,* the *Turkey,* the *Haut-bois,* or high-stalked, and many others, some of which are white, and some of so deep a red as

to approach towards a black. To say which sort is best is very difficult. A variety of sorts is best.—They are propagated from young
plants that grow out of the old ones. In the summer the plant sends
forth *runners.* Where these touch the ground, at a certain distance
from the plant, come roots, and from these roots, a plant springs up.
This plant is put out *early* in the fall. It takes root before winter; and
the next year it will *bear a little;* and send out runners of its own.—
To make a Strawberry-bed, plant three rows a foot apart, and at
8 inches apart in the rows. Keep the ground clean, and the new
plants, coming from runners, will fill up the whole of the ground,
and will extend the bed on the sides.—Cut off the runners at six
inches distance from the sides, and then you have a bed *three feet
wide,* covering *all the ground;* and this is the best way; for the fruit
then lodges on the stems and leaves, and is not beaten into the dirt
by heavy rains, which it is if the plants stand in clumps with clear
ground between them.—If you have more beds than one, there
should be a clear space of two feet wide between them, and this
space should be well manured and deeply digged every fall, and
kept clean by hoeing in the summer. If weeds come up in the
beds, they should be carefully pulled out.—In November the leaves
should be cut off with a scythe, or reap-hook, and there should be
a little good mouldy manure scattered over them.—They will last
in this way for many years. When they begin to fail, make new beds.
Supposing you to have five or six beds, you may make one new one
every year and thus keep your supply always ample.

324.

VINE.

See *Grape.*

325.

WALNUT.

The butter-nut, the black walnut, the hickory or white walnut,
are all inhabitants of the American woods. The English and French

Walnut, called here the *Madeira Nut,* is too sensible of the frost to thrive much in this climate. Two that I sent to Pennsylvania in 1800 are alive, and throw out shoots every year; but they have got to no size, their shoots being generally cut down in winter.—Walnuts are raised from seed.—To preserve this seed, which is also the fruit, you must treat it like that of the *Filberd,* which see.—It is *possible,* that the Madeira Nut grafted upon the black walnut, or upon either of the other two, might thrive in this climate.

VI

FLOWERS.

OF FLOWERS, AND OF ORNAMENTAL GARDENING IN GENERAL.

326.

My reason for making *Flowers* a part of my subject, have been stated in Paragraphs 6 and 97. However, if the American Farmer have no taste for flowers, his wife and daughters may; and this part of the book can, at any rate, do him no harm.

327.

Under the head of Flowers come flowering *trees* and *shrubs;* and, therefore, I must, in this place, say a little of these and of ornamental gardening. It is by no means my intention to attempt to give an account of *all* the flowers that come into the florist's catalogue. That catalogue, with only a very short description of each flower, would fill ten volumes, each surpassing this in bulk. I do not blame the taste of those who study *botany,* and who find pleasure in the possession of *curious* trees and plants; but, all that I shall attempt, is, to speak of those flowers that stand most prominent as to their capacity of making a *beautiful show* and of sending forth *fragrance.*

328.

As to the *spot* for flowers, the smaller kinds, and even small shrubs, such as roses, dwarf honeysuckles, and the like, may be planted by the sides of the broad walks in the kitchen garden, or, a little piece of ground may be set apart for the purpose. In cases where there are what are usually called *pleasure-grounds*, large shrubs, and, if the grounds be extensive, lofty trees come in. And, in the placing of the whole of the trees and plants, the most lofty should be farthest from the walk.

329.

As to the manner of sowing, planting, transplanting, and cultivating, what has been said of fruit trees and of garden vegetables and herbs applies here. The ground must be *good*, well tilled, and kept clean, or the plants and flowers will not be fine.

330.

Before I proceed to the *Alphabetical List*, let me again observe, that I merely give a *selection*, such as appears to me to be best calculated for gratifying, at different seasons, the sight, or the smell, or both. That there is a great deal in *rarity* is evident enough; for, while the English think nothing of the *Hawthorn*, the Americans think nothing of the *Arbutus*, the *Rhododendron*, the *Kalmia*, and hundreds of other shrubs, which are amongst the choicest in England. The little dwarf brush stuff, that infects the plains in Long Island under the name of *"Kill-Calf,"* is, under a fine *Latin* name, a choice greenhouse plant in England, selling for a dollar when not bigger than a handful of thyme. Nay, that accursed stinking thing, with a *yellow* flower, called the *"Plain-Weed,"* which is the torment of the neighbouring farmer, has been, above all the plants in this world, chosen as the most conspicuous ornament of the front of the King of England's grandest palace, that of Hampton-Court, where, growing in a rich soil to the height of five or six feet, it, under the name of *"Golden Rod,"* nods over the whole length of the edge of a walk, three quarters of a mile long and, perhaps thirty feet wide, the most magnificent perhaps, in Europe. But, be not too hasty, American, in laughing at John Bull's king; for, I see, as a choice flower in *your* gardens, that still more pernicious European weed, which the French call the *Coquelicot*, and the English, the *Corn-Poppy*, which stifles the barley, the wheat, and especially the peas, and frequently makes the fields the colour of blood.

331.

This is quite sufficient to show the power of *rarity* in affixing value on shrubs and flowers. The finest flowering trees and shrubs in England have been got from America. The *Wild Cherry*, which they call the *bird-cherry*, which here grows sometimes to the height of a hundred feet and one of which I can now see from my window more than seventy feet high; the *Locust*, most beautiful of trees and best of timber; the *Catalpha*, blossoms far more beautiful than those of the horse-chestnut, broad and beautiful leaves that do not scorch in the hottest sun; all the beautifully blowing *Laurel-tribe*; the *Rose of Charon* (as it is called here) and the *Althea Frutex*; the *Azalia* of all colours; *Roses* of several kinds. But, there is one shrub of the larger kind, abundant here, that I never saw there, and that is the thing which some call the *Morning Star*. It has six leaves in its flower, which is in the form of the flower of the *single rose*. The whole flower when open, is about *three times the circumference of a dollar*. Some of the trees bear blossoms quite white, and others blossoms of a whitish peach blossom colour. These blossoms come the *earliest* in the spring. They are out *full*, in Long Island, in the first week in *May*, which is rather earlier than the peach-blossoms. In England, they would be out full, on an average of years, in the *last week of February*, which is an anticipation of all their shrubs. The trees, which is a great quality, thrive well *under other trees*, which, indeed, seems to be their nature. You see, from a great distance, their bright and large blossoms, unaccompanied by leaves, shining through the boughs of the other trees; and some of them reach the height of *forty feet*. This, therefore, is a very fine flowering tree; and yet I never saw one of the kind in England. How beautiful a grove might be made of this tree, the wild-cherry, the Locust, the Catalpha, and the Althea-frutex! And here they are all, only for the trouble of *sowing;* for from the seed the tree will surely come.

332.

I shall now proceed to give an Alphabetical List of such flowering Trees, Shrubs, and Plants, as I think worthy of cultivation; or, rather, that I myself would wish to have about my house, or in my garden. As I go on I shall state some particulars here and there relating to propagation and management: but, to be very particular would be superfluous, seeing that such full directions have been given in the former parts of the work, as to the sowing of all seeds, great as well as small; as to the raising of trees and plants from cuttings, slips, layers and suckers, and as to cultivation and tillage. Flowers are divided into *annuals, biennials* and *perennials.* The first blow and die the year they are sown; the second blow the second year and then die; the third sometimes blow the first year and sometimes not, and die down to the ground annually, but spring up again every spring. I have not made separate lists; but have included the whole in one Alphabetical List. There are sixty trees, shrubs, and plants altogether; and, if properly cultivated, these will give a grand bloom from May to November.

LIST.
333.

ALTHEA FRUTEX.

It is raised from seed, or from suckers. There are several sorts, as to colours. They should be mixed to make a variety. Save the seed in November or December. The pods are full. Sow in the spring.

Seed produces the handsomest shrub; and it is to be got almost any where.

334.

ANEMONE.

This is a very beautiful flower, and worthy of great pains. It is raised from seed, or from pieces of the roots. Sow the seed in spring. The plant does not blow the first year. The root, which is *tuberous,* is taken up in the fall, dried in the sun, and put by in the dry till spring, when it is put into the ground again. And, during the summer, it sends out young roots, which must be taken off and planted out, to become *blowers.* There is a great variety of colours and of sizes of this flower.

335.

ARBUTUS.

A pretty ever-green, as well known as the oak tree; and is to be got every where.

336.

ASTRE (CHINA.)

Astre is French for *star,* and this flower, in its shape, resembles a star to our view. It is *annual,* bears great quantities of seed, and is sown early in spring. An infinite variety of colours, and great quantities of blossoms. It gives no smell; but a clump of it furnishes a great mass of beauty to the sight.

337.

AURICULA.

This is one of the flowers, the sorts of which are distinguished by having awarded to them the names of famous *men* and *women,* famous *cities,* and famous *battles,* and so forth. It may be raised from seed; but the flowers proceeding from plants so raised, do not resemble the flowers of the mother plant, except by mere accident. It is a chance if you get a *fine flower* from a whole sown bed. Now-and-then one of this description comes, however, and this adds to the list of *names,* if it happen to be one of the like of which has not made its appearance before. Auriculas are, therefore, propagated by parting the roots, and every root sends out several young plants annually. When sown, they do not blow till the *second year;* but the old root lasts for many years. Some of these should be *potted,* and kept to blow in the green-house. If planted in the natural ground, they ought to be covered a little in the winter. There are many hundreds of sorts with *names.* So many indeed, that the godfathers in England have been so put to it for great personages to baptize the flowers after, that they have been compelled to resort to the heroes and heroines of Romance; accordingly they have *Don Quickset* and *Sancho.* However vanity supplies the florists, as well as the shipowners, with a great store of *names,* and auriculas, like ships, are very frequently honoured with the names of the original proprietor's wife or daughter.

338.

AZALIA.

That little American Honeysuckle that impedes our steps when shooting on the skirts of woods. It however, blows profusely, though it has no smell like the English honeysuckle.

339.

BALSAM.

Balsam is an *annual* and a most beautiful plant, with great abundance of flowers. Sow when you sow Melons, at a distance of four feet; leave only one plant in a place; let the ground be rich and kept clean; it will blow early in July, and will keep growing and blowing till the frost comes, and then, like the cucumber, it is instantly cut down. I have seen Balsams in Pennsylvania 3 feet high, with side-branches 2 feet long, and with a stem much bigger than my wrist, loaded with beautiful blossoms. Plant, branch, leaf, flower; all are most elegantly formed, and the colours of the flower extraordinarily vivid and various. There are, however, some more *double* than others, and some variegated. The seed of these should be sowed, and it comes in great abundance. The flower of the Balsam has no smell.

340.

BRIAR (SWEET.)

A well known shrub of the *rose* kind. Bows of it carefully planted and pruned make very good hedges, and it will grow in almost any ground, though fastest in good ground.

341.

CAMILLIA.

This shrub, which is of the *laurel-tribe,* has lately been introduced in England from Japan. It bears a flower, which, when open, resembles a good deal a large full-blown rose; and these flowers, on different plants, are of different colours. It is raised, doubtless, from seed; but it may be *grafted* on the *Hawthorn;* and, I dare say, on the *Crab.* Some of the plants have been sold at 20 or 30 pounds each. By this time they are probably sold at a dollar. The plant as well as the flower are handsome; and certainly *cuttings for grafting* may easily be brought from England. They will stand the winter as well as any of the American laurels.

342.

CARNATION.

Here is beauty and fragrance, and both in the highest degree. There are various sorts, distinguished, like those of the Auricula, by *names;* and, what is said of the seed of the Auricula applies here. If sown, the carnation does not blow till the second year. It is usually propagated by *layers.* While it is blowing, it sends out several side shoots near the ground. These are pinned down, in *August,* to the earth with a little stick with a hook at the end of it. A little cut, or tongue, is made on the under side of the shoot; and thus the head of the shoot is brought upright. The part that touches the ground is well covered with earth; and *roots* come out here before the fall. Then the stalk, which connects the young plant with the old one is cut off; the young plant is transplanted, and the next year it blows. The old root does not stand another year well; and, therefore, its branches are thus made use of to keep up the race and the sort.—Carnations are rather tender as to frost. And must be well covered in this country to live through the winter. It is best to put them in large pots to give room for *laying;* and to keep them in a green-house in winter, or in some house, where they can have sun and air. However, they merit all the pains that can be bestowed upon them.

343.

CATALPHA.

That beautiful American tree mentioned in Paragraph 331.

344.

CLOVE.

Is only a more handy and less esteemed sort of *Carnation,* which see. It may be propagated like the Carnation; or, by *cuttings,* which is the easier way. Instead of *laying* down the side shoots, you cut them off. Then you cut away the *hard* part of the shoot, strip off three or four of the bottom leaves. *Tip* the rest of the leaves; make a little split in the butt of the shoot, and, then, with a little smooth pointed stick, plant the cutting in the ground. This is to be done early in August. The young Cloves will have roots in the fall; and you may transplant them into the open ground or into pots to blow the next year. The old Clove plant will, however, blow for many years. I should think, that, with good covering, such as directed for *spinach,* Cloves would live out the winter in this country.

345.

COLUMBINE.

A *perennial.* Very common; but very pretty.

346.

COWSLIP.

This is one of the four flowers, without which English pastoral poetry would be destitute of that which awakens the most delightful ideas. The *Cowslip,* the *Primrose,* the *Violet,* and the *Daisy,* are of endless recurrence in that species of writing. They all come early in the spring; and are all beautiful. Neither of them is seen here, and they all might; for they will bear any severity of weather. The Cowslip is of the *Polyanthus* tribe. It is of a delicate yellow colour, and sends forth many blossoms from the same stem, which rises about six inches from the ground. It may easily be propagated from seed, which it bears in great abundance, but, when you once have a plant, the easiest way, is to propagate from *offsets.* The plants raised from seed do not blow till the *second year.* The plant is *perennial.* The flower has a delicate sweet smell, and also sweet taste, as a proof of which, cart-loads of the flowers, plucked from the stalks, are sold in London to make *"wine"* with; that is to say, to furnish drinkers with an apology for swallowing spirits under the specious name of Cowslip-wine. The leaf of the flower very much resembles in shape the under lip of a *cow,* whence, I suppose, our forefathers gave the plant the name of cowslip.

347.

CROCUS.

A bulbous rooted plant, very well known. It is recommended by its *earliness.* It is perfectly hardy. The only thing to do when it is once planted, is to take care that it does not fill all the ground near it. There are yellow, blue, and white Crocuses. And they are pleasant when nothing else is in bloom, except, at least, the *Snowdrop,* which departs soon after the Crocus begins to appear.

348.

DAISY.

I cannot say, with Dryden's damsels, in one of his fine poems, that "the Daisy *smells so sweet,*" for it has very little smell; but it is a most beautiful little flower, and blows without ceasing at all times when the grass grows, however little that may be. The opening of the Daisy is the sure sign that there is growth going on in the grass; and these little flowers bespangle the lawns and the meadows, the green banks and the glades all over England. Their colours present an endless variety; and those grown in gardens are double. The field-Daisy is single, and about the size of a York Six-pence. Those in the gardens are sometimes as broad as a quarter of a dollar. And there is one other sort called the *Hen-and-chicken* Daisy, that has a ring of little flowers surrounding the main flower. This plant may be raised from offsets or seed, in which last case it blows the second year. It is perennial.

349.

GERANIUM.

Geranium wants *hardiness only* to make it the finest flower-plant of which I have any knowledge. Some give us flower with little or no leaf; others have beauty of leaf as well as of flower, but give us no fragrance; others, like the rose, give us this added to beauty of flower and of leaf, but, give us them only for a part of the year. But, the Geranium has beautiful leaf, beautiful flower, fragrant smell from *leaf as well as from flower,* and these it has in never-ceasing abundance; and as to *variety of sorts,* as well as in leaf as in flower, it surpasses even the flower of the Auricula. How delightful the country, where Geraniums form the underwood, and the Myrtles tower above! Softly, my friends. Beneath that underwood lurk the poisonous lizards and serpents, and through those Myrtle boughs the deadly winged adders rustle; while all around is dry and burning sand. The Geranium is a native of the South of Africa; and, though it will not receive its death-blow from even a sharpish frost, it will not endure the winter, even in the mild climate of England. But, then, it is so easy of cultivation, it grows so fast, blows so soon, and is so little troublesome, that it seems to argue an insensibility to the charms of nature not to have Geraniums if we have the means of obtaining earth and sun.—The Geranium is propagated from seed, or from cuttings. The seed, like that of the Auricula, does not produce flower or leaf like the mother plant, except by chance. It is easily saved, and for curiosity's sake, may be sown to see if a new variety will come. But, a cutting, from any part of the plant, old wood or young wood, stuck into the ground, or into a pot, will grow and become a plant, and will blow in a month from the time you put it into the ground. You must have plants, indeed, to cut from; but these may be, in small number at any rate, in a window during winter. When the spring comes, cut them up into cuttings, put these in the ground where you wish to have plants during the summer. They will be in bloom by July, and, before October, will be large as a currant tree. Take off cuttings from these during September, put them in pots, and they are ready for the next spring. If you have a *Green-house*, you have Geraniums in full bloom all the long dreary winter.

350.

GUELDER-ROSE.

This is called here the *Snow-ball tree*. It is raised either from layers or suckers. Its bloom is of short duration; but, for the time, makes a grand show in a shrubbery. The suckers of it ought to be dug clean away every year.

351.

HAWTHORN.

This tree has been amply described in Chapter I, under the head of Fencing. Sometimes it is called Hawthorn, and sometimes White-thorn.

352.

HEART'S-EASE, OR *PANSEY.*

A beautiful little *annual,* which has great varieties, and all of them pretty. It blows all the summer. It may be sown in the fall, without any care about covering the ground; but, it must not *come up,* in this country, till spring.

353.

HEATH.

The common English heath is hardy, but ugly. The *Heaths* from Africa are of infinite variety. Insignificant in flower, however, and must be housed in Winter. They are propagated from seed, or from slips, and will last a long while. A few in a green-house are pretty; and they look gay in winter.

354.

HOLLYHOCK.

This is a fine showy plant for a shubbery. There are double and single, and none but the double should be cultivated. It may be raised from seed, or from offsets. If the former it does not blow till the second year. It will remain in the ground many years, and is perfectly hardy.

355.

HOLLYHOCK (CHINESE.)

This is a more tender and far more beautiful kind than the common. It is raised from seed only; blows the second year, and *only* that year. It is, therefore, a *biennial.*

356.

HONEYSUCKLE.

This, amongst all English shrubs, is the only rival of the Rose; and, if put to the vote, perhaps as many persons would decide for the one as for the other. Its name indicates its sweetness of *taste,* and the smell is delightful almost beyond comparison. The plant is also beautiful: it climbs up houses and over hedges; it forms arbors and bowers: and has a long-continued succession of blossoms. It grows wild in all parts of England, in many parts covering the hedges and climbing up the trees. There is little variety as to sorts. That which is cultivated has a larger and deeper-coloured bloom, but the wild has the sweetest smell.—It *may* be propagated from seed; but always *is* from cuttings; put into the ground in the spring, and treated like other wood-cuttings. See Paragraph 276.

357.

HYACINTH.

This is a *bulbous-rooted* plant, and, like all the plants of that class, is *perennial*. It may be raised from *seed;* but, as in the case of the Auricula and many other plants, it is many chances to one, that, out of a whole bed, you do not get a good flower; and, perhaps, it is a hundred to one that you do not get a flower to resemble the mother plant. Therefore, none but curious florists attempt to raise from seed. The roots are propagated from off-sets; that is to say, the mother root, while it is blowing, sends out, on its sides, several young ones. The old root, young ones and all, are put away in a dry place, out of the reach of severe frost, till spring. Then, when you plant the old one out to blow again, you take off the young ones and plant them also. They do not blow the first year, and, if weak, not the second. But, in time, they do; and then they produce offsets. This is the way the Hyacinth is multiplied. It is a fine and fragrant flower; it blows early, and will blow well even in glasses in a room; but better in earth. A fine flower for a green-house, where it would be out in full bloom while the snow was on the ground.

358.

JASMIN.

Has the merit of a very delightful smell, and that only. Its leaf and flower are insignificant. It climbs, however, and is good to cover bowers. It is easily raised from *cuttings*. See Paragraph 276.

359.

JONQUIL.

An elegant and sweet smelling bulbous rooted plant. Propagated, and cultivated, in all respects, like the *Hyacinth*, which see.

360.

KALMIA.

An evergreen shrub of great beauty, and of several varieties, great quantities of which are seen in most of the rocky woodlands of this country.

361.

KILL-CALF.

Mentioned in Paragraph 330, which see. It is a dwarf shrub, and may be raised from seed, or from suckers. It is very pretty. When in bloom it resembles a large clump of Sweet Williams. It is so pretty that it is worth having in the green-house, where it would blow, probably in April, in Long Island.

362.

LABURNHAM.

This is a tall and beautiful shrub, loaded, when in bloom, with yellow blossoms, in chains; whence it is sometimes called the *Golden Chain*. I sent one out to Pennsylvania in 1800; but, though *alive* now, it has never got to any height, and has never borne blossoms, being continually nipped by the winter. That it will grow and thrive in this country is, however, certain; for I saw two very fine trees in grand bloom in the garden, between *Brooklyn* and the Turnpike gate, last spring. It is raised from the seed as easily as Indian Corn is.

363.

LARKSPUR.

An *annual* of no smell, but of great variety as to colours, and when in a clump, or bed, presenting a great mass of bloom. There is a *dwarf* and a *tall* sort. The dwarf is the best. There is a *branching* kind, which is good for nothing.

364.

LILAC.

Desirable for its great masses of fine large bunches of bloom. There is the White, the Blue, and the Reddish. It is propagated from *suckers*, of which it sends out too many, and from which it should be kept as clear as possible. It is an ugly shrub when out of bloom. The leaves soon become brown. Therefore, there should be but few Lilacs in a shrubbery.

365.

LILY OF THE VALLEY.

This the only Lily that I should like to have. It is a pretty little dwarf plant, that thrives best in the shade, where it produces beautiful blossoms of exquisite sweetness. It is a *bulbous root*, and propagated from offsets.

366.

LOCUST.

Well known, and sufficiently noticed in Paragraph 331. It may be raised from *suckers;* but best from *seed*, which always makes the *straightest trunk*.

367.

LUPIN.

A species of *pea* or *tare*, and frequently cultivated in the fields, and eaten in soup and otherwise, by the Italians, and in the South of France. It grows, however, upon a stiff stem, and is upright, and branches out, like a tree in miniature. There is a great variety of sorts, as to colour of flower as well as to size of plant. The *Yellow dwarf* is the best, and it smells very sweet. This plant is, of course, an *annual*.

368.

MAGNOLIA.

One of the finest of the *laurel* tribe. It can be raised from seed, or from *layers*. A very fine shrub indeed. There are several varieties of it.

369.

MIGNONETTE.

An *annual* that bears abundance of seed. The plant and the flower do not surpass those of the most contemptible weed; but the flower has a very sweet smell. It may, if you have a green-house, be had at any time of the year. The plants may stand at four or five inches asunder; but, if they stand thicker, the bloom is inferior, and does not last so long.

370.

MORNING STAR.

This fine shrub has been sufficiently described in Paragraph 331. It can be raised from seed, or from layers.

371.

MYRTLE.

The Myrtle is a native of climates where it is *never cold*. It will not endure even November *all out,* in Long Island. To have it, therefore, it must be housed in winter. It may be raised from seed, cuttings, slips, or layers. The leaf of the Myrtle has a fine smell; and, when the tree is in bloom, it is pretty. But, it is a *gloomy looking shrub.* One Geranium is worth a thousand Myrtles. The broad-leaved Myrtle is the best in every respect, and especially because it is easily brought to *blow.*

372.

NARCISSUS.

A bulbous-rooted plant, managed precisely like the *Hyacinth,* which see. It blows early, is very beautiful, and has a delightful smell. Nothing is easier than the propagation and management of flowers of this tribe, and few are more pleasing. The Narcissus is a very nice thing for a parlour, or a green-house.

373.

PASSION-FLOWER.

So called because the flower has a *Cross* in the middle, and *rays,* resembling *a glory,* round the edges of it. It is a singularly beautiful flower. The plant is also beautiful. It is a *climber,* like the Honeysuckle; and, like that, has a succession of blossoms that keep it in bloom a long while. It is raised from *cuttings,* which, treated as other cuttings are, easily take root.

374.

PŒONY.

A *perennial* that may be raised from seed or offsets. A grand flower for shrubberies. Each flower is usually as big as a tea-cup, and one plant will sometimes produce twenty or thirty.

375.

PEA (SWEET.)

There are a great variety in the *annual* sorts as to colour of blossom, and, there is a *perennial* sort, called *everlasting pea*. This stands, of course, year after year. The others are sown and cultivated like the common garden pea. They should have some sticks to keep them up. This is a very *showy* flower, and remains in bloom a long while.

376.

PINK.

This flower is too well known to need describing here. There are a great variety of sorts, as to the flower; but all are cultivated in the same way; exactly as directed for the *Clove*, which see. The Pink root will last a great many years; but, the flower is seldom so fine as the first year of the plant's blowing.

377.

POLYANTHUS.

Every thing that has been said of the *Auricula* (which see) may be said of the Polyanthus. It is a very pretty flower, and universally esteemed. It blows finest out of the *hot* sun. Polyanthuses are best in *beds;* for a great part of their merit consists of the endless *variety* which they present to the eye. The Polyanthus has a delicately sweet smell, like that of the Cowslip.

378.

POPPY.

A very bad smell, but still is to be sought for on account of its very great variety in size, height, and in flower; and on account of the gayness of that flower. The seed pods of some are of the bulk of a three pound weight, while those of others are not so big as even a small pea. The smallest, however, contains about a *thousand seeds,* and these come up, and the plants flourish, with very little care. A pretty large bed, with two or three hundred sorts in it, is a spectacle hardly surpassed in beauty by any thing in the vegetable creation. It is an *annual,* of course. It is well known as a *medicinal* plant; but, it is not so well known as a plant from the seed of which *sallad-oil* is sometimes made! The Germans, on the Rhine, cultivate whole fields of it for this purpose. It may be as well, therefore, for us to take care not to use German Sallad-Oil, which, however, can with great difficulty be distinguished from oil of olives.

379.

PRIMROSE.

A beautiful little flower of a pale yellow and delicate smell. It comes very early in the spring; and continues a good while in bloom. Of the fibrous rooted flowers it is the next to the Daisy in point of earliness. It is a universal favourite; and, in England, it comes abundantly in woods, pastures and banks. It is *perennial* like the *Cowslip,* and is propagated in the same manner. How beautiful a Long Island wood would look in *April,* the ground beneath the trees being decked with Primroses!

380.

RANUNCULUS.

Is a flower of the nature of the *Anemone,* which see. It is propagated and cultivated in the same manner. These two flowers are usually planted out in beds, where they make a very fine show.

381.

RHODODENDRON.

It never occurred, perhaps, to any American to give this fine name to the laurel with a long narrow leaf and great bunches of blue, pink, or white flowers, the balls, or pods, containing which, appear the year before the flower. It is, however, a beautiful shrub, and not less beautiful on account of its frequently covering scores of acres of *rocky sides of hills,* or on account of English Gardeners believing that it requires *bog-earth* (though fetched from many miles distance, at vast expense) to make it grow and blow!

382.

ROSES.

A volume larger than this would not describe the differences in all the sorts of this, which has, for ages, been considered as the Queen of Flowers, the excellences of which to attempt to describe would be to insult the taste of every reader. I shall, therefore, merely speak of the propagation and the management of the plant. All roses *may* be propagated from *seed;* but, as the seed seldom comes up till the *second year,* and as the plants come to perfection slowly, the usual mode of propagation of all sorts, except the *China Rose,* is by *suckers.* These come out near old stems, during the summer; they are dug up in the fall and planted out. In the spring they are cut down near to the ground, and, the next year, they blow.— The *China Rose* is so easily raised from *cuttings,* that little bits, put in the ground in spring, will be trees, and have a profusion of bloom before the fall. This Rose is in bloom, in England, from *May till January,* if the soil and situation both be good.—It is very strange that Mr. MARSHALL should set this down amongst *"tender shrubs,"* and say, that "it will not do *abroad,* except in the *summer months."* It stands the winter as well as the *oak,* and, I have, for years, had it, against the front of my house, *blowing finely at Christmas,* without any attempt at covering. In America, in the open air, it might not be in *bloom* at Christmas; but it stands the winter as well as any tree that can be named. It is beautiful for the Green-house; for there it, mixed with Geraniums, blow beautifully all the winter long. As to the management of roses; the ground should be good, and dug every autumn as directed for fruit trees, and should be manured frequently. They should (except when trained against walls or over bowers) be kept cut down *low;* for, when they get long stems and limbs, they, like peach trees, not only look ugly, but bear but few flowers, and those very mean ones. They should, therefore, be cut to within a foot, or less, of the ground; and all dead or weak wood should be pruned out close, without leaving any ugly stubs.

383.

SIBERIAN CRAB.

This Shrub is, by some, esteemed for its *fruit*, of which they make a conserve, more, I imagine, to gratify the sight than to gratify the palate. But, as a *tall shrub*, it yields, for the time, to very few. There is the red-blossomed and the white-blossomed. The branches of both, when in bloom, present ropes of flowers, while the trunk, the limbs, the branches and the leaves, are all delicate in form and in hue.

384.

SNOW DROP.

The *earliest* of all flowers. In England it blows in January. Once in the ground it is not very easy to get it out again. Nothing but *carrying it away*, or actually consuming it with fire will rid you of it. No sun, not even an American sun, will kill a Snow-Drop bulb, if it *touch the ground*.

385.

STOCK.

There are *annuals* and *biennials* of this name; and, if I were to choose amongst all the annuals and biennials, I should certainly choose the *Stock*. Elegant leaf, elegant plant, beautiful, showy, and most fragrant flower; and, with suitable attention, bloom, even in the natural ground, from May to November in England, and from June to November here.—The annuals are called *ten-week* Stocks. And of these there are, with a peagreen leaf, the *Red, White, Purple,* and *Scarlet,* and, then, there are all the same colours with a Wall-flower or Sea-Green *leaf.* So that there are *eight* sorts of the annual

Stock.—Of the *biennials,* there are the *Brompton,* of which there are the *Scarlet* and the *White;* the *Dutch,* which is *Red;* the *Queen's,* of which there are the *Red* and the *White;* and the *Twickenham,* which is *Purple.*—As to propagation, it is, of course, by *seed* only. If there be nothing but the natural ground to rely on, the sowing must be early; the earth very *fine* and very *rich.* The seed is small and thin, and does not easily come up in coarse earth. If the plants come up thick, thin them, when very young. And do not leave them nearer together than six inches. They, however, *transplant very well;* and those that have not place to blow in may be removed, and a *succession* of bloom is thus secured. If you have a green-house, glass frame, or hand-glass, you get flowers six weeks earlier.—The *biennials* are sown at the same time, and treated in the same way. They blow the *second year;* but, if there be great difficulty in preserving them, in the natural ground, through the winter in England, what must it be *here!* Indeed, it cannot be done; and yet, they are *so fine;* so *lofty;* such masses of beautiful and fragrant flowers; and they continue so long in bloom, that they are worth any care and any trouble. There is but one way: the plants, when they get ten or a dozen leaves, must be put into flower-pots. These may be sunk in the earth, in the open ground, till November (Long Island,) and when the sharp frosts come, the pots must be taken up, and placed *out of the reach of hard frost,* and where there is, however, *sun and air.* When the spring comes, the pots may be put out into the natural ground again; or, which is better, the balls of earth may be put into a hole made for the purpose; and thus the plants will be *in the natural ground to blow.* In this country they should be placed in the *shade* when put out again; for a very hot sun is apt to tarnish the bloom.

386.
SYRINGA, OR *MOCK-ORANGE.*

A very stout shrub, with blossoms much like that of the orange, and with a powerful smell. It is propagated from suckers, of which it sends out a great many.

387.

SWEET WILLIAM.

A very pretty flower. Makes a fine show. Comes Double by chance; and is very handsome whether double or single. It is propagated from seed, the plants coming from which do not blow till the *second year*. The Sweet William root does not last many years. It *may* be propagated by parting the roots; and this *must* be done to have *the same flower again to a certainty*, because the seed do not, except *by chance*, produce flowers like those of the mother plant.

388.

TUBEROSE.

This is a bulbous-rooted plant that sends up a beautiful and most fragrant flower. But, even in England, it cannot be brought to perfection without artificial heat in the spring. If got forward in a green-house, or hot-bed, and put out about the middle of June, it would blow beautifully in America. It is a native of Italy, and the roots are brought to England and sold there in the shops. It is propagated and managed precisely like the *Hyacinth,* which see.

389.

TULIP.

Beds of Tulips vie with those of *Carnations* and *Auriculas.* They are made *shows* of in England, and a single root is sometimes sold for two or three hundred guineas. And, why not; as well as make shows of *pictures,* and sell them for large sums? There is an endless variety in the colours of the tulip. The bulbs, to have the flowers fine, must be treated like those of the *Hyacinth.* The tulip may be raised from *seed;* but it is, as in the case of the Hyacinth, a thousand to one against getting from seed a flower like that of the mother plant.

390.

VIOLET.

This is one of the four favourites of the Spring in England. It is a little creeping plant, that comes on banks under the shelter of warm hedges. The flower is so well known to excel in sweetness, that, *"as sweet as a violet"* is a phrase as common as any in the English language. There is a *purple* and a *white.* Abundance of seed is borne annually by both; and the plant is perennial. If you propagate from seed the flower does not come till the second year; but, one plant, taken from an old root, will fill a rod of ground in a few years.— There is a little plant in these woods in Long Island, with a flower precisely like that of the purple violet; but, the leaf is *a narrow oblong,* instead of being, as the English is, in the shape of a heart; the plant does not creep; and the flower has *no smell.*

391.

WALL-FLOWER.

It is so called, because it will grow, sow itself, and furnish bloom in this way, by a succession of plants, for ever, upon old walls, where it makes a beautiful show. It bears abundance of seed, plants from which produce flowers the second year. Some come *double,* sometimes. If you wish to be sure of double flowers, you must propagate by slips of double-flowering plants. There are the *yellow* and the *mixed,* partly yellow and partly red. All have a delightful smell, blow early, and are generally great favourites. I am afraid this plant, even with covering, will not stand the winter out of doors in America, unless in the south front of a building, and *covered too* in severe weather; for, even in England, it is sometimes killed by the frosts.

INDEX

To Vegetables and Herbs, Fruits and Flowers.

VEGETABLES AND HERBS.

	Paragraph.		Paragraph.
Artichoke	192	Chervil	211
Asparagus	193	Cives	212
Balm	194	Coriander	213
Basil	195	Corn	214
Bean	196	Corn-Salad	215
Bean (Kidney)	197	Cress (Pepper Grass)	216
Beet	198	Cucumber	217
Brocoli	199	Dandelion	218
Burnet	200	Dock	219
Cabbage	201	Endive	220
Calabash	202	Fennel	221
Cale	203	Garlick	222
Cale (Sea)	204	Gourd	223
Camomile	205	Hop	224
Capsicum	206	Horse-Radish	225
Caraway	207	Hyssop	226
Carrot	208	Jerusalem Artichoke	227
Cauliflower	209	Lavender	228
Celery	210	Leek	229

Paragraph.

Lettuce	230
Mangel Wurzel	231
Marjoram	232
Marigold	233
Melon	234
Mint	235
Mustard	236
Nasturtium	237
Onion	238
Parsley	239
Parsnip	240
Pea	241
Pennyroyal	242
Pepper—see Capsicum.	
Pepper-grass—see Cress.	
Potatoe	245
Potatoe (Sweet)	246
Pumpkin	247
Purslane	248
Radish	249
Rampion	250
Rape	251

Paragraph.

Rhubarb	252
Rosemary	253
Rue	254
Ruta-Baga—see Turnip.	
Sage	256
Salsafy	257
Samphire	258
Savory	259
Savoy	260
Scorzenera	261
Shalot	262
Skirret	263
Sorrel	264
Spinach	265
Squash	266
Tansy	267
Tarragon	268
Thyme	269
Tomatum	270
Turnip	271
Wormwood	272

FRUITS.

Apple	300
Apricot	301
Barberry	302
Cherry	303
Chestnut	304
Cranberry	305
Currant	306
Fig	307
Filberd	308
Gooseberry	309
Grape	310
Huckleberry	311
Madeira Nut—see Walnut.	

Medlar	313
Melon	314
Mulberry	315
Nectarine	316
Nut	317
Peach	318
Pear	319
Plums	320
Quince	321
Raspberry	322
Strawberry	323
Vine—see Grape.	
Walnut	325

FLOWERS.

	Paragraph.		Paragraph.
Althea Frutex	333	Larkspur	363
Anemone	334	Lilac	364
Arbutus	335	Lily of the Valley	365
Astre (China)	336	Locust	366
Auricula	337	Lupin	367
Azalia	338	Magnolia	368
Balsam	339	Mignonette	369
Briar (Sweet)	340	Morning-Star	370
Camillia	341	Myrtle	371
Carnation	342	Narcissus	372
Catalpha	343	Passion-Flower	373
Clove	344	Pœony	374
Columbine	345	Pea (Sweet)	375
Cowslip	346	Pink	376
Crocus	347	Polyanthus	377
Daisy	348	Poppy	378
Geranium	349	Primrose	379
Guelder-Rose	350	Ranunculus	380
Hawthorn	351	Rhododendron	381
Heart's-ease (Pansey)	352	Roses	382
Heath	353	Siberian Crab	383
Hollyhock	354	Snow Drop	384
Hollyhock (Chinese)	355	Stock	385
Honeysuckle	356	Syringa (Mock Orange)	386
Hyacinth	357	Sweet William	387
Jasmin	358	Tuberose	388
Jonquil	359	Tulip	389
Kalmia	360	Violet	390
Kill-calf	361	Wall-Flower	391
Laburnham	362		

INDEX

To the General Matter.

[The Figures refer to the Paragraphs, and not to Pages.]

Paragraph

Addison... 121

Boxes, earthen-ware preferable to, for plants 109
Bacon, Lord.. 121

Cultivation, in general... 126, 176
    as relates to Fruits 291
Curwen, Mr. John Christian... 183
Cowley 121

Drilling, mode of... 162, 163
Diseases of Trees.. 298
Dryden 348

Fencing 30
    for shade and shelter 33, 48
    expense of... 47, 50, 51

Paragraph

    seed for, how to procure..55

    Quick-set, described..39

Garden, its praises, the produce and pleasures derived from 2, 3, 121

Green-houses 97

    the usefulness of 100, 117, 118, 121

Girard, Mr. Stephen 308

Hot-beds...63

    frames for common in America....................................71

    hand-glasses useful 94

Herbs, preserving and forcing of them 117

Hampton Court, vine at..310

    flowers at 330

Hulme, Mr. 310

Laying out of gardens...57

Le Gau, Mr..310

Lucerne, depth of its roots 193

Loves of the plants 141

Manures...28, 29

Missing, Mr...188

Marshall, Rev. Mr..................................... 145, 281, 282, 382

McAllister, Mr. 55

Planting...283

Propagation in general 125

    as relates to fruits...273

    of cuttings 276

    of slips...277

Propagation of layers 278

    suckers 279

    grafting 281

    stocks...282

Paul, Messrs.. 282, 308

Paragraph

Situation for a garden 12
Soil 16
Sowing 155
    and planting in pots . . . . 110 to 114
Seed, sorts of 128
    when true 129
    when sound 131
    saving and preserving of 136
    table of duration of 150
Sorts of plants, error respecting changes of 188
Setting of fruit, an erroneous notion . . . . 141 to 145

Trenching, best mode of 20
Transplanting 169
Temple, Sir William 122
Tull, Mr. . . . . 182 to 183

Roots, to find their length horizontally 184

Walls, not necessary for fruit 32
Watering of plants, not recommended 187
Women, duly appreciated in America 101

WILLIAM COBBETT, born in Surrey in 1762, was a muckraking British journalist, the most prolific of his age, and the publisher of *The Political Register,* the main newspaper of the working class in early-nineteenth-century England. Famous under his pseudonym Peter Porcupine, he was a brilliant satirist with a gift for inspired ridicule. He was imprisoned at Newgate for sedition and libel various times in his life and spent a two-year exile on Long Island, in New York, during which he leased a farm and wrote a grammar of the English Language in addition to *The American Gardener.* He is the author of many books, including *Rural Rides,* which champions traditional rural England against the changes wrought by the industrial revolution. He was elected to the House of Commons at the end of his life, before his death in 1835.

A NOTE ON THE TYPE

The principal text of this Modern Library edition
was set in a digitized version of Janson, a typeface that
dates from about 1690 and was cut by Nicholas Kis,
a Hungarian working in Amsterdam. The original matrices have
survived and are held by the Stempel foundry in Germany.
Hermann Zapf redesigned some of the weights and sizes for
Stempel, basing his revisions on the original design.